ARIZONA
Mogollon Rim

TEXT BY DON DEDERA

ILLUSTRATIONS BY BILL AHRENDT
PHOTOGRAPHY BY
ARIZONA HIGHWAYS CONTRIBUTORS
DESIGN BY GARY BENNETT

ARIZONA HIGHWAYS
BOOKS

Produced in cooperation with the
United States Forest Service

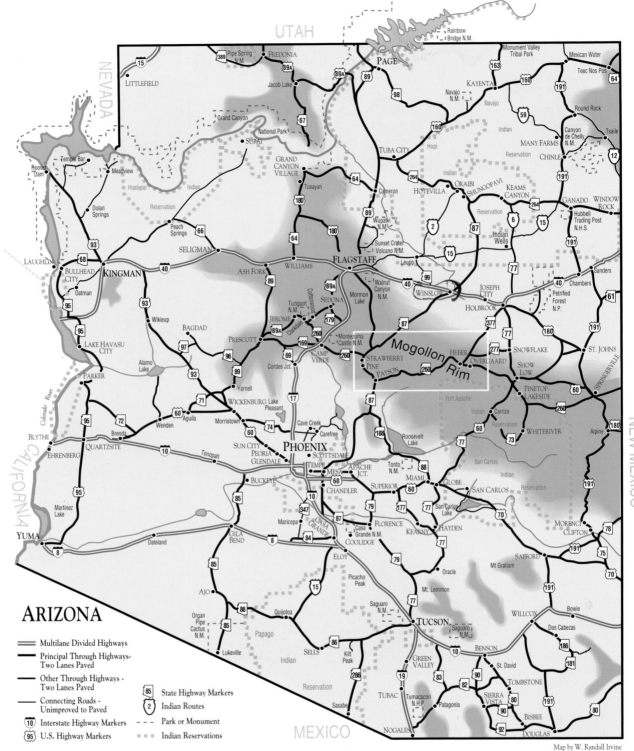

ARIZONA

Map Legend:
- ═══ Multilane Divided Highways
- ━━━ Principal Through Highways-
  Two Lanes Paved
- ── Other Through Highways -
  Two Lanes Paved
- ── Connecting Roads -
  Unimproved to Paved
- (10) Interstate Highway Markers
- (95) U.S. Highway Markers
- (85) State Highway Markers
- (2) Indian Routes
- - - - Park or Monument
- ▪▪▪▪ Indian Reservations

Map by W. Randall Irvine

Arizona's Mogollon Rim Published by the Book Division of *Arizona Highways* magazine, a monthly publication of the Arizona Department of Transportation, 2039 West Lewis Avenue, Phoenix, Arizona 85009. Telephone: (602) 712-2200 Web site: www.arizonahighways.com

Win Holden—Publisher   Bob Albano—Managing Editor   Evelyn Howell, P.K. McMahon—Associate Editors
Mary Winkelman Velgos—Art Director   Peter Ensenberger—Photography Director   Cindy Mackey—Production Director

Contents

Flinging before it sizzling bolts of lightning, a summer thunderstorm marches across Tonto Basin en route to the Mogollon. FRANK ZULLO

Introduction

A s a young boy I was brought to Arizona by a father seeking relief from cruelly painful arthritis. Our move came only a short spell after the American Southwest's own adolescence. A baker's dozen of us Boy Scouts — chaperoned by a schoolteacher at the wheel of a borrowed, battered school bus — had made camp at Grand Canyon, and now we were drifting homeward. Half my companions were impoverished Pima Indians whose forebears, as volunteer militia, scouted and routed enemy renegade Indians.

Back then, there were Boston suburbs containing more citizens than all of Arizona. In 1940, the federal census enumerated 499,261 residents. If Arizonans were sprinkled over the map evenly like shaken pepper, only four people would occupy a square mile. About half of Arizona's people in those days huddled together in three or four towns, and counties bigger than Connecticut counted populations the size of a large high school.

On our return trip, we very nearly reduced Arizona's population by 14.

Our bus was one of those 1930-something lemon yellow pumpkins with a high center of gravity and oily brakes. Of course,

The Mogollon Rim Country

A WORLD APART

there were no seat belts. Our gear, including geology samples, canned goods, and iron cookware, was stowed in the overhead book racks. About 10 miles southwest of Long Valley, the unpaved washboard logging road reached the abrupt edge of the regional Colorado Plateau. Conifer-clad, the Mogollon Rim at that point rises some 8,000 feet above sea level, and the angle of repose approximates 90 degrees — meaning that toward the center of the planet, the force of mass for ages had relentlessly tugged. So

(RIGHT) An Aphrodite butterfly pauses to perch upon a Rim country wildflower.
FRANK ZULLO
(LEFT) A morning campfire perfumes the clear air of a Rim's-edge campsite.
NICK BEREZENKO
(FOLLOWING PANEL) Crimson box elders burst into autumn dress, while quaking aspens have nearly spent all of their golden dollars.
LARRY ULRICH

everything loose (including buses) tended to slip and congregate as detritus upon the shaky alluvial fans which buttressed vertical cliffs.

In the 1880s when Revilo (Oliver spelled backward) Fuller freighted this hill, he would fell a virgin ponderosa pine, chain the bole to his rear axle, and drag it down the 1,000-foot drop to Strawberry village. This kept his wagon from overrunning his team. On the extremely steep grades, he would slip logs through the spokes to lock the wheels. In the 1940s, this road was not much improved since it was surveyed by Fuller's mules.

Well, we pitched off the Rim piloted by our teacher, who was accustomed to driving the level desert at Casa Grande. (Geographically speaking, Casa Grande could serve as proper headquarters for the International Flat Earth Society.) We hit the first turn about 20 mph too fast, as simultaneously we boys made a rush to the right side for an eagle's view of Strawberry Valley. The driver jumped the brakes hard, a shoe grabbed, tires slid, and a solid ton of boys pressed against the glass. The bus nearly swapped ends, while our Feather Merchant driver spun the wheel in the manner of playing bumper tag in a carnival ride. Somehow we didn't tip as the tires flipped gravel over the edge. And by some miracle, our helmsman wrenched the vehicle into a right bend carved out of a sedimentary shelf. Unsheathed axes, tents, and all manner of camping gear cascaded from the overhead racks onto our heads. Thirteen lads thereupon fell as sodden dolls against the *left* window panes, to watch a hundred yards of limestone slide by, six inches from our noses. Our teacher never did gain full control of the bus until we arrived in the swale of Strawberry.

White as bone, the teacher trembled out of the door and went inside a small store that displayed an

A-1 Beer sign. We kids stood around. After a long absence, our teacher eventually emerged with an armload of frosty Barqs strawberry drinks. I detected on his breath a certain yeasty aroma.

Twenty miles more down the road, with crimson tongues and a goofy professor, we eased into Payson, a false-front cowtown beside itself with the "August Doin's" — that was rodeo, as authentic as it was in the early days. Bulldoggin'. Steer ropin'. Horse races on Main Street. Pretty girls in tight Levi's. Genuine cowboys.

Such was my introduction to the Rim country. And may this anecdote help to explain why, a half-century later, when people ask about my feelings for this country, I tell them I love the Rim the way a poor, scared, dry-mouthed boy off the alkali desert loves an ice-cold Barqs soda pop on a summer day.

With the exception of the Grand Canyon, Arizona's most impressive landform is the Mogollon Rim. It scribes the abrupt southern edge of the vast, four-state Colorado Plateau. Geologist Halka Chronic tells us:

"Here on the Colorado Plateau a great block of the earth's crust has remained coherent and recognizable through 600 million years and more, while blocks around it have been tilted and squeezed and broken. . . . There seems to be some sort of underlying difference here, a difference that has lasted through much of the earth's history, as if the more or less circular patch of the earth's crust that makes up the Plateau obeyed a different set of geologic rules."

Starting in far northwestern Arizona and angling to a point south of Flagstaff, sheer cliffs begin to show themselves in the Sycamore Canyon and Oak Creek Canyon areas. The Rim then curves east by southeast more than 200 miles and extends well into New Mexico as the Mogollon Mountains. All along this sharp crustal edge, Mother Earth parades a combination of typical features: relatively flat plateau cut by north-flowing streams . . . near-vertical cliffs dropping hundreds of feet . . . then a jumble of steep-sloped talus and massif drained by a series of watercourses running generally south and west.

So formidable is this escarpment, it was given wide berth by intrepid Spanish soldiers and priests who otherwise busily poked around the region during the two centuries preceding the founding of the United States. Of this fastness, a 50-mile-wide heartland was not much populated until the 1960s, '70s, and '80s. Even today, after the growth of the 1990s, Payson's residents number fewer than 15,000.

The Rim is named for Juan Ignacio Flores Mogollon, governor of New Mexico which, in the early 1700s under Spanish rule, included Arizona. According to Delia Sanchez, teacher of Spanish at Phoenix Community College, the proper articulation of Mogollon is "Mo" (as in mow the grass), "go" (the g hard as in the English "go"), and the last syllable an accented "YAWN" (as when you're sleepy). Self-appointed Spanglish authority, folklorist James E. Cook, declares that the most common *norteamericano* rendition is "Muggy-OWN," as in, "It's *muggy* today, and I'm glad I *own* a cabin on the Rim."

This middle section of the Mogollon now and then goes by another, more easily pronounced nickname, the Tonto Rim, or simply, "the Rim." This highland occasionally is called Zane Grey Country.

The most popular Western novelist before Louis L'Amour, Grey frequently retreated to his Arizona cabin during the first decades of the 20th century. Virtually roadless woodlands lay all about. Grey would recline in an overstuffed chair on a porch that hung like a scaffold over the Tonto Basin. Needing scenic description, he could lower his paper and absorb vistas of cotton cloud, endless forest, and steel-blue mountains.

"Westward along the Rim vast capes jutted out, differing in shape and length, all ragged sharp, fringed, reaching darkly for the gold and purple glory of the sunset. Shafts and rays of light streamed from the rifts in the clouds, blazing upon the rock faces of the wall. Eastward the Rim zigzagged endlessly into pale cold purple. Southward a vast green hollow ran like a river to the sea, to empty, it seemed, into space. Beyond that rose dim spectral shapes of mountains, remote and detached. To the north the great wall shut out what might lie beyond. . . ."

Today, Zane Grey Country is made more accessible by modern highways, but it remains much as it was when it inspired such sagas as *To the Last Man* and *Under the Tonto Rim*. By foresight and good fortune, the priceless qualities of the Rim largely have been preserved as national forest.

Gone are the Indian hunters, the hard-riding dragoons, the Spanish seekers of mineral riches, the wagon trains of settlers, the pioneer ranchers, the lonely shepherds, and the first of America's ecologists, federal foresters.

This is still the refuge of elk, deer, bear, and lion. You yet may ride a mount all day through certain of the Rim's mountain passes and never cross a paved road. The adventurous hiker can tackle a 50-mile-long trail with sure knowledge he will not smell engine exhaust fumes anywhere along the way.

In the Rim country, history buffs can retrace the expeditions of early-day beaver trappers, stand at the site of an Indian massacre, touch the walls of a long-ago homestead, or visit the graves of victims of a bloody range war. The Rim country is a land big enough to welcome birdwatchers, picnickers, painters, campers, gem seekers, fishermen, and a few tired souls who simply want to withdraw to a sylvan glade.

Recently, the sentiment was voiced by a gent who retired and moved to Arizona from Delaware, where the highest elevation is Jerimoth Hill, 812 feet above sea level. At first sight, this newcomer bought a house in Payson, spent more than a summer exploring the country within a 50-mile radius, and bragged in a letter home:

"Folks, I didn't just buy a cabin. I bought a whole country!" ⚑

RICK ODELL

Scottsdale free-lance writer, Don Dedera, a former editor of *Arizona Highways* magazine, has been writing about Southwestern subjects for more than 40 years. His works include a thousand non-fiction articles and 15 books, notably *A Little War of Our Own*, about a violent range feud that blazed through the Rim country in the late 1800s. Many of his essays cover the Rim and Payson, where he and his wife, Nancy, make their second home.

Chapter One

T he Mogollon Rim country!

Where in the West does a place contain more reality and romance of the 19th century's American frontier?

Here survive remnant forts from the Indian wars, honest-to-gosh working cow ranches, trails blazed by army scouts and mountain men, and, against all odds, humble log cabins made comfortable by industrious settlers in olden days. Here, too, dwell descendants of Arizona's first pioneers, great-grandchildren of wagon train immigrants. And caretakers of artifacts left by ancient cultures, the U.S. Cavalry, Apache braves, gold prospectors, six-gun sheriffs, saloon girls, schoolmarms, and officers' ladies.

Here three thriving national forests contribute sweeps of woodland to form the Massachusetts-sized portion called the Mogollon Rim. For fortunate moderns, the Rim takes in a piece of outdoors with room enough for wilderness backpacking, ritual flyfishing, nature filming, back road four-wheeling, overland skiing, productive gem-seeking, roadside picnicking, hobby gardening, rock climbing, and just plain stumpsitting.

Bigger, this area is, than many countries of the world. And if the Rim country really were a country, the piney town of Payson would be its capital.

Located near the geographical center of Arizona, Payson today is reached by several easy ways. But the most popular is State Route 87, often referred to locally as "the Beeline Highway." State Route 87 is a logarithmic improvement over the rutted wagon path of the 1880s and a hundred times better than the dusty car road of the 1950s that could consume six hours and two tires in the drive from Phoenix.

Payson, as a modern American settlement, goes back not much more than a century, but about 1,500 years ago, the town's site was home for a prehistoric people archaeologists call the Mogollon Culture.

Payson

GATEWAY TO THE RIM COUNTRY

Thus far, approximately 50 archaeological sites have been identified within 2,000 acres of Tonto National Forest surrounding Payson.

As an engaging reminder of the first Americans, at Payson's southern entrance today prospers one of Arizona's smaller Indian

(LEFT) With State Route 87 pointing to the Rim on the horizon, Payson casually sprawls out into groves of ponderosa, piñon, and oak.
MICHAEL COLLIER
(RIGHT) Toes start tapping to the irresistible dance tunes of Payson's Old-Time Fiddlers Contest, which celebrates a rich musical heritage.
JEFF KIDA

reservations. The Tonto Apaches for nearly a century were dispossessed squatters, facing day-to-day eviction. In 1972, Congress set aside a desirable juniper-studded hillside to be the Tonto Apache Indian Reservation. Today, the tribe participates in Payson events and operates several enterprises, including the Mazatzal Casino.

The first whites to see the region were soldiers on campaign and prospectors seeking gold and silver. By now, the Athabascan Apaches considered the Rim their motherland. Undeterred, William Burch, miner-rancher, operated the Golden Waif Mine in the area as early as 1878 and erected a stout cabin in 1883 on what is now Burch Mesa, near today's Payson Airport. Burch's brand served as the only place name for a while.

Nearby rises the remains of Fort McDonald, a stone-encircled hilltop fortified in 1878 as a community retreat during Indian uprisings. As settlement slowly increased, the place was known as Green Valley, then as Union Park, and, since March

3, 1884, as Payson, in honor of the Illinois senator who helped the village obtain a post office.

Impulse and derring-do continue as Payson traditions. One legendary example was after a double wedding, when the parties filed out of the office of the Payson justice of the peace one August day in 1890. Local frontiersman Arizona Charlie Meadows bellowed:

"It is my pleasure to offer, as my present to these newlyweds, that if all the parties in attendance will saddle up with their lariats and ride over my ranges, the brides and grooms can have any of my unbranded calves you can catch!"

(ABOVE) Costumed mountain men enliven Payson's rodeo parade. (OPPOSITE PAGE, LEFT) A crosscut sawyer competes in a logging festival. (TOP RIGHT) An Apache Crown Dancer leads the way. PHOTOS BY NICK BEREZENKO (LOWER RIGHT) Arizona Charlie Meadows grew his hair long for a career in Wild West shows. COURTESY SHARLOT HALL MUSEUM, JEAN KING COLLECTION

Rodeo! By the time the chaotic calf scramble concluded at dusk, more than 30 head of Charlie's dogies had been roped and branded as starter stock for the two couples.

While Tombstone made news as Shoot-'em-up Junction, early Payson was more noted for good-natured drinking and dancing than street fighting. As historian Marguerite Noble has written:

"Although Payson was not an unruly pioneer town, the saloons were highly patronized and often incited commotion. Rambunctious drunks were chained to a tree to sleep off their problems. The settlers were mainly peaceable families, colonizing and stabilizing new borders, but they were neither timid nor cowardly when the need came for them to take care of themselves.

"Jake Lane, a newcomer from Texas, left one of the saloons after an excessive drinking bout. He rode up and down the street, shooting his pistol. Myrle Evans and Myrth Jones, now 82 . . . say they were playing croquet with their friends when Jake ran his horse through their game 'scattering us like quail.' [One of the players was Judge William Colcord.] The judge advised Jake to put away his little shooter. Instead Lane pointed his gun at William Colcord. This was a mistake — and his last. Guns blasted. Lane toppled from his horse, dead from Colcord's Luger. The court cleared Colcord."

But for such an infrequent exception, a heritage of spontaneous generosity continues to permeate Payson's lifestyle. Hitchhikers wait not long. Payson drivers tend to wave at every other car. They blast their horns at friends. Western dress prevails: cowboy boots

or hiking boots, everywhere denims. Maybe a Lexus some day will sell in the Payson area, but not until it's offered in a four-wheel-drive pickup truck configuration.

The ranching image is bona fide. Only in recent times was Payson encircled by the town fence to prevent range cattle from browsing the flower beds. But still at risk are vegetable gardens and orchards, routinely harvested by deer, javelina, and (look out!) a mama black bear with cubs. Unplanned in the totally planned Payson West development: On a recent morning the half-devoured remains of a coyote were found encircled by cougar tracks.

Now that the sawmill is closed, Payson's laid-back citizens continue ranching or making a living in tourism, manufacturing, services, and light industry. Local cottage factories thrive, producing everything from whatnots to whirligigs. At times it seems half of Payson buys the other half of the town in interlocking swap meets, only to advertise the junk for sale the following weekend. Subdivisions proliferate to shelter retirees and second-home owners (both working class and wealthy; Payson has an impressive number of million-dollar homes.)

An accelerating number of Rim country workers are flextimers and telecommuters, those home-based high techs who could live anywhere they might plug in their computer, fax, and modem. Some holidays Payson's resident population of about 13,180 (as of 1999) swells to maybe 20,000 flatland "furriners," counting those out camping in the woods.

Busier by the day is Payson's improved airport, with a 5,500-foot runway, ample taxiways, and paved aircraft parking area. The restaurant is a popular fly-in-for-breakfast spot, especially on weekends, and about 50 private aircraft make Payson their home base.

No doubt the air was intoxicating as wine before Payson was settled. It's as clean today as then, except for wintry morns when wood stove smoke lingers in the still pockets of air. In fact, *Sunbelt Retirement Magazine* identified Payson as one of the three healthiest places in the world to live, thanks to having one of only three Pure Ozone Belts in the world. Payson's mild, four-season climate typifies Arizona at about a mile high: temperatures averaging 15 to 20 degrees cooler than the deserts; an average 21 inches of annual precipitation, most falling between November and March. Three or four substantial snowfalls below the Rim usually melt swiftly, although at higher elevations a snowpack can last for weeks and months.

(LEFT) When the thunder gods stage electrical extravaganzas atop the Rim north of Payson, it's time to hurry home and huddle inside a cozy cottage or cabin.
TOM BEAN

Celestial fireworks dominate the skies through July and August and into September as masses of moist air push northward from Mexico and ram into the Rim. During the summer rainy season at any time, but usually between midday and 3:00 P.M., cumulonimbus clouds boil to 40,000 feet and both entertain and astound with one of earth's superlative lightning displays. Psychedelic flashes, rolling bombinations, and drenching downpours scrub the skies. More than 200,000 lightning bolts were recorded during one Arizona August, the greater number striking along the Rim.

So, where does the newcomer begin enjoying Payson?

Main Street — The town boasts that all other chambers of commerce pale in comparison to Payson's friendly ways, and impressed visitors have assured me that this is not empty bragging. The tiny chamber of commerce anchors the north side of Main Street at the first traffic signal in the south section of town. Maps, brochures, advice, plain and fancy brags, gossip, and corn relish recipes available. Be sure to drop by.

If parts of Payson's Main Street seem like movie sets, well, they have been used as such. Spirited horses of the Houston brothers used to sprint from the schoolhouse to the sawmill for as much as $1,200 on a side. The oldest building in Payson huddles as a small adobe back of the Olla Lazear home. It was built for a Mr. Siddles by a Mr. Vogel for $30 in 30 days. Other structures along Main Street have been cataloged in an effort to qualify the street for the National Register of Historic Places.

Rumsey Park — This popular public park offers lighted ball fields; basketball, shuffleboard, and tennis courts; and an Olympic-size swimming pool. From the junction of State Route 87 and State Route 260, take Overland or Longhorn roads west to McLane Road, then go north about half a mile on McLane.

Green Valley Park — The town built Green Valley Park in 1996. Its three mandmade fishing lakes are sustained with reclaimed water, which then is "leaked" to recharge the groundwater supply. Graced with grassy banks and shade trees, park facilities include a fishing dock and boat ramp. The Rim Country Museum is nearby.

The Rim Country Museum — Look for the sign reading "Home of Northern Gila County Historical Society Payson Museum." Dedicated in 1990, the Rim Country Museum (sometimes still called the Museum of the Forest) preserves two buildings important to the area: the original Forest Service Ranger Station and the ranger residence. Obtained together with the site by an act of Congress, the museum is owned and administered by the historical society. The two older buildings have been lovingly restored.

A unifying structure reminiscent of Payson's burned down Herron Hotel stands between the old frame edifices. The new museum houses public exhibits ranging from Zane Grey's saddle to historic quilts and an old sawmill. Displays are changed often.

Unique perhaps, and nifty as a perfect antique can be, stands the top 25 feet of the Forest Service lookout tower salvaged from the apex of Mount Ord south of Payson. It had been assembled in the 1930s by the Civilian Conservation Corps. The fire tower is outfitted with fire-sighting instruments, period telephone, and other apparatus used by lookouts to spot and report wildfires through more than 50 years.

Payson's festivals — Expressed in its motto, "the festival capital of Arizona," Payson fills the calendar with weekend events. Most notable are the "August Doin's," the festivities surrounding the Payson rodeo, acknowledged as the Annual World's Oldest Continuous Rodeo. Since 1882 — even during World War II — Payson has hosted the event, and the rodeo enjoys official sanction by the Professional Rodeo Cowboys Association.

Into its third decade, the Payson Old Time Country Music Festival attracts pickers and grinners from everywhere. On other occasions, Payson hosts a junior rodeo, a chili cook-off, numerous arts and crafts shows, a square dance extravaganza, and a Christmas lighting ceremony centered around the alpine-like Swiss Village.

So Payson's future seems as promising as its past was productive. With its spirit of community intact, it will always be a place for visitors to kick back and relax, or get up and go, as in the days when Zane Grey himself played and worked and wrote, under the "Tonto Rim." ⊻

(ABOVE, LEFT) Payson Junior Rodeo is only one of the town's several cowboy tournaments.
(ABOVE, CENTER) High-stepping western dancers keep time to fiddle music.
(ABOVE, RIGHT) Calf roping, Junior Rodeo style.
PHOTOS BY NICK BEREZENKO

W H E N Y O U G O . . .

Payson offers rustic inns and modern motels, eclectic eateries and fast-food drive-ins along State 87/260. Or stock up at the local specialty shops and supermarkets.

Rim Country Regional Chamber of Commerce
Payson branch.
(520) 474-4515 or
(800) 672-9766.

The Rim Country Museum
(formerly the Museum of the Forest) Green Valley Park, 700 Green Valley Parkway, Payson.

(520) 474-3483. Open Wednesday through Sunday, noon to 4 P.M. Admission.

Green Valley Lakes
Green Valley Park, one mile west of State 87, Payson.
(520) 474-5242, Ext. 7. With urban fishing license, fish sunrise to 10:30 P.M. No swimming or wading.

Tonto Apache Tribe
For information on tribal events, call the tribal office, (520) 474-5000. Casino, (520) 474-6004 or (800) 777-PLAY.

Payson Ranger District
(Tonto National Forest) State 260, one mile east of State 87, Payson. (520) 474-7900.

The Rim Country Museum.
NICK BEREZENKO

THE SAGA OF LEO THE LION

If Hollywood had scripted it for a fictional movie, critics would have mercilessly panned the plot, to wit:

MGM's Leo the Lion attempts to fly coast to coast.

Crashes in a Payson wilderness.

Lives to roar 10,000 times.

Thanks to cowboys who rescued him.

Plot thins. Totally lacks a love interest.

But this was not a film; rather, a bold quest of publicity. And as such, it deserved an Oscar. In fact, the entertainment journal *Variety* dubbed it "the most sensational exploitation stunt ever done in the motion picture industry."

Gruff, cigar-chomping movie mogul Louis B. Mayer complained that things were a little slow at Metro-Goldwyn-Mayer in 1927. America's passion for movies was being overtaken by fascination with flying, popularized by the solo nonstop Atlantic flight of Charles A. Lindbergh.

"Let's fly Leo coast to coast nonstop," suggested publicity director Peter Smith (remember his zany short features, the Pete Smith Specials?).

So over the objections of animal rightists, 350-pound Leo was placed inside a 400-pound steel-and-glass cage encased within the fuselage of a high-wing Ryan Brougham. With barnstormer Martin Jensen at the controls and the 220-horsepower engine revving over the red line, the monoplane wobbled off an airstrip near San Diego September 16.

Somehow Jensen conquered the Laguna Mountains, traversed the deserts. He refueled in Phoenix and even negotiated a pass in the Mazatzal Mountains. But nearing the narrowing end of Hells Gate Canyon, he realized *no way* did he have the power to climb over the Mogollon Rim dead ahead. So 15 miles east of Payson, with no room to turn around, he stalled the aircraft into a large clump of oak trees, which absorbed most of the energy of the crash. Jenson suffered a cut over his eye. Leo and Leo's cage: miraculously unhurt and intact.

The pilot walked nearly three days southwestward before running into George Booth near the hamlet of Gisela. When the word got out, the rescue of Leo focused the nation's full attention.

People and equipment mustered at Kohl's Ranch before trucking into Bear Flat. A 15-member party of mostly cowboys went horseback to the crash site, some six straight-line miles, but 12 roundabout. There they found Leo hungry and thirsty, but strong enough inside his cage to be loaded onto a makeshift travois. A skittish team of mules, urged on by Leo's scent and growls, dragged the sled out to the road at Bear Flat. There the cage was loaded onto a truck for transport to Payson.

While regaining his strength, the king of beasts delighted the children of Payson and grabbed headlines around the world.

In time, Leo went home. He never flew again, thereby foregoing an untold fortune in frequent flyer credits. 🐾

Chapter Two

Pine & Strawberry

TWINS AMONG THE TREES

While Payson's connection to the Rim is that of a tidewater town not far from the coast — the ocean is *over there* five leagues — Pine and other small communities beneath the Rim insert themselves right into it, as tiny harbors tucked into a rocky, wave-lashed headland. The Rim is no rumor for the town of Pine. For Pine, the Rim serves as its own enormous shore of a landlocked archipelago. All about, as in Zane Grey's imagery, unbroken woodlands, like a verdant, bounding main, extend outward to empty beyond lost horizons.

To a traveler approaching it, the Rim seems slowly to ooze up from the primal basements of the planet, to block out the lower third of the sky. As you draw closer, the Rim asserts itself as sheer towers forming recesses, points, and promontories. Bare rock pokes through the forest in rainbows of warm hues. As often as not, soft white or menacing cobalt clouds decorate a firmament so clear and baby blue it breaks your heart. Eagles in updrafts polish limey brows averaging 7,500 feet above sea level. As the gargantuan hulk leans on the human psyche, time slows to the syncopated clopping of the hooves of a walking cow pony. This is ranching country, relaxing country, wave-through-the-windshield country, unlocked-door country.

After Capt. John G. Bourke negotiated the crest of the Rim in 1871, he described it as "a strange freak of nature, a mountain canted up on one side." Another Arizona author, Charles Bowden, wrote of the Mogollon Rim 110 years later:

"Here the edge of the great stone wafer to the north slowly erodes backward into itself and spills soil onto the deserts below. The dissolving edge pulsed with periods of uplift, warped with faulting, and wound up higher than either the plateau to the north or the deserts to the south. The lip has shed the more

(OPPOSITE PAGE) A tiny enclave clings to a meadow at the edge of the frosty forest at Strawberry.
(RIGHT) Keepsake of a pioneer family, an antique buggy wears wintry decor at Pine. PHOTOS BY NICK BEREZENKO

recent rock of the geologic clock and is down to Precambrian stone, material a billion or two years old."

From Payson, State Route 87 heads northwest and soon tacks down and up the canyon of the East Fork of the Verde River. Enroute to Pine, you'll pass several points of interest that are worth a look.

Flowing Spring — Forest Service Road 272, four miles up State Route 87 from Payson, strikes sharply to the right and down to the East Verde River. About any car can survive the washboard roadbed, and you'll arrive at a concrete ford connecting grassy flats and deciduous arbors on both sides of the river for two miles. It's an ideal family area with a shallow stream for wading. Except on holiday weekends — when it's so crowded that you have to pack in your own rock to sit on — this is a great camping area.

East Verde Park — A quarter mile farther up State Route 87 where the highway crosses the river, FR 622 heads downstream to East Verde Park. Probably more rainbow trout have been caught in this stretch of stream than anywhere else along the Rim. The park ranks as one of the region's favorite picnic spots. And on holidays, ditto the crowds.

Tonto Natural Bridge — Northwest of Payson 9.5 miles, a dead-end, graded and graveled road runs three miles west to the bridge. What a surprise David Gowan got in 1877 while prospecting Pine Creek for precious metals. He didn't find his fortune, but he claimed discovery of the world's largest travertine arch — a stone bridge 183 feet high over a 400-foot-long tunnel that is 150 feet wide. You can gasp at his discovery when you visit Tonto Natural Bridge State Park.

Geologists say it took Pine Creek a million years to deposit and sculpt calcium carbonate into today's massive span. During frontier times, a five-acre dairy thrived on its top. By some accounts, Gowan, a longtime saltwater sailor, initially explored the expansive caverns by swinging himself from side to side on ropes like a pendulum.

In 1927, Gowan's relatives erected a 10-room lodge, which was once architecturally described as "Staunch American Utilitarian." But the place is homey and, now refurbished as the park's visitor center, is open to daytime tours, except when groups reserve the lodge for overnight stays or conferences and receptions. The lodge's setting is charming with its hidden valley, spring, waterfall, and old fruit orchard. Pioneer Andrew Ogilvie built the swimming pool with a team of four horses pulling a scoop shovel. The park is open every day, and there is an admission charge.

Pine was settled in 1879 by disciples of the Church of Jesus Christ of Latter-day Saints. The Mormon influence remains much in evidence — a tidy church and community center rather typical of western Mormon towns. Today,

(LEFT) From this viewpoint at Tonto Natural Bridge, visitors can feel the tunnel's cool, fresh air fanning their faces.
WESLEY HOLDEN
(OPPOSITE PAGE, TOP) Pools, grottoes, and racing rapids grace the landscape near Second Crossing on the East Verde River.
PATRICK FISCHER
(OPPOSITE PAGE, FAR RIGHT) Soaking up the rays and cooling off near Flowing Springs on the East Verde.
WESLEY HOLDEN
(OPPOSITE PAGE, RIGHT) The historic Tonto Natural Bridge Lodge.
TOM BEAN

descendants of founders share space with retirees, summer-heat refugees, and spirited young people. Some two dozen subdivisions tucked among the pines and junipers bear names like Berry Hill, Eagle Glen, and Canyon Shadows.

Along the main street and by woodsy lanes with casual fence lines, Pine stitches together a loose scatter of antique shops, old farm homes, specialty stores, and service establishments. Here and there a stone or log hut dating to the early days is embraced

by a larger, more modern house. Following a wet spring, yards bloom with the old-fashioned flowers: hollyhocks, asters, and daisies. When Pine stages its down-home Northern Gila County Fair in September, exhibits vary from beef jerky to needlework, wild grape jam, sunbonnets, bola ties, and Big Max pumpkins.

During summer weekends, the Pine/Strawberry Museum exhibits Indian and pioneer artifacts and historical photographs. Local pioneer families have donated most of the exhibits — heirlooms and whatnots that tell Pine's and Strawberry's history. You can find the museum at Pine's community center just off the highway.

In common with the rest of the Rim country, Pine's climate challenges prediction. At 5,400 feet, Pine perches 400 feet higher than Payson. In early spring and late fall, that's high enough to turn Payson drizzle into Pine sleet. And one May day you could savor the chef's special in The Rim Cafe while a brisk snow shower slants past the windows. Deep snowpacks some years persist atop the Rim while the first catch of squash and beans sprouts in Pine's backyard patches.

"We can follow the seasons by what falls on our heads," says artist Bill Ahrendt. "One month the pine needles descend, and another brings a rain of tiny worms. The oaks lose their leaves in the spring, and there are times when there's so much pollen, it coats everything like volcanic ash.

"And smells. You can close your eyes and still perceive the doings of Mother Nature. On a nice warm day when the sap is running, you can go up to one of those old ponderosa pines, put your arms around it and bury your nose in one of those yellow streaks in the bark, and inhale the most delicious fragrance of sugary butterscotch. Yes, butterscotch."

A distinguished teacher as well as a draftsman and painter, Ahrendt adjudges the Rim's residents and visitors to have an artistic streak: "We don't qualify as a colony, but there are enough enclaves of artists, artisans, and patrons to lend a measure of culture to our communities."

To prove the point, annual arts and crafts events customarily bring together 30 to 50 Rim country artists and artisans, running the gamut from classical egg tempera painting to keen custom knife-making.

And if you lack an artistic streak, the wealth of local wildlife just might inspire one. Larry Toschick, an internationally known artist who for 16 years painted wildlife at his home near Pine, counted 45 species of birds on his lot. Now a desert dweller for health reasons, Larry pines for Pine "and its incredibly rich variety of species. The raptors are wonderful: Cooper's, sharp-shinned and sparrow hawks, as well as the common red-tailed. You'll see flocks of band-tail pigeon, choirs of several kinds of warblers together, and pairs of sandhill cranes. They are God's gifts."

Strawberry, the hamlet in its namesake valley, lies three miles northwest of Pine. At 6,800 feet elevation, another notch up the climatological ladder, Strawberry can copy Maine while Payson feels like Mexico. Strawberry measured six feet of snow on the level in December, 1967, and four feet in two days in February, 1986. But during some winters, snowfall is light.

Go 1.6 miles west of State Route 87 on the Fossil Creek Road, and you'll spot the Strawberry Schoolhouse, Arizona's oldest standing schoolhouse, now restored and equipped in original condition. The one-room school was built in 1885 of huge, squared pine logs, its interior finished elegantly — for its time — with wallpaper and paneled wainscoting, testimony to the yearning for education on the raw frontier. The local historical society opens the schoolhouse for public tours and summer cultural activities. One weekend there may be a music event, another, demonstrations of period arts and crafts.

Strawberry residents tend hobby farms and orchards, pen pet horses, and trade in real estate. Out on the highway, little businesses like Lonnie's Enchanted Cottage cater to tourists. Breakfast at the Strawberry Lodge continues a tradition older than granite. Sportsman's Chalet across the street boasts the only elevator in town — a dumbwaiter that lifts drinks to the pool shooters on the second floor.

If trails were freeways, the Pine-Strawberry area would make a world-class interchange. Hiker's heaven. Options galore. At the Pine Trailhead at the south end of Pine, take your pick from the Pine Canyon Trail, Donahue Trail, Oak Springs Trail, and the old Highline Trail (see map on pages 32-33).

Hugging the base of the Rim from Pine to State Route 260 east of Christopher Creek, the Highline long served pioneers as a transportation and commercial link across this rugged land. You can hike, ride horseback, or mountain bike the Highline's 51-mile entirety, camping along the way. Or, since

roads cross it at convenient intervals, divide it into day hikes. Located at about 5,500 feet elevation, the Highline is a year-round trail only occasionally closed by snow. Vegetation ranges from cactus and manzanita to piñon and juniper to ponderosa pine and fir. The trail crosses a number of perennial streams and offers spectacular views of the Rim above and the basins and ranges below.

For back country explorers, perhaps the greater harm inflicted by the Dude Fire of 1990 was the charring of the very heart of the Highline. Until the Dude, the Highline was vegetated for nearly all of its length. The fire took out the 17-mile central section from Dude Creek to the Tonto Creek Fish Hatchery. The Highline Trail is still walkable end to end — and deer, elk, and other wildlife thrive on the new grasses — but that central section will take a century and more to regain its before-the-fire appearance.

But if something less strenuous is your style, the unfailing thrill of Strawberry is driving the

(OPPOSITE PAGE) "Out to feed the horses, "
South Road, Pine.
Nick Berezenko
(ABOVE) Readin', writin', 'rithmetic, and
restoration at the Strawberry Schoolhouse.
Bob and Suzanne Clemenz
(LEFT) Ralph Fuller and Bill Barcus run a batch
of apple cider through a relic press.
Nick Berezenko

ascent/descent of State Route 87 between the lodge and the Rim. On top, more than one traveler has likened the stunning panorama of Strawberry Valley to "standing on the edge of the earth." That is where, incidentally, a certain school bus almost sailed off long, long ago.

You can double back (take it easy!) through Pine and about two miles south to an unpaved gravel track wending eastward, the Control Road (FR 64).

There, at the Control Road/State Route 87 intersection, sprawls an excellent hunting ground for fossils of shellfish and other denizens of the deep — evidence that these mile-high mounts once formed the bottom of a sea. Rockhounds consider the Rim country to be a mineralogist's dream-come-true. Chert, quartz, and gem-quality geodes are plentiful. Just about any prospector or rock shop can put you onto a scatter of handsome red jasper or agate.

The Control Road, built by the CCC to help suppress wildfire, is not designed for a fast pace. It bends through slopes bristling with cactus patches and spear-shaped succulents, ferns and forbs, through prime specimens of what botanists call the Transition Zone: that contour of climate neither arid nor alpine, a land of thrifty piñon pines and alligator juniper, of stubborn barberry bush and fine-leaf yucca, perennial bunchgrass and annual wildflowers, of gnarled manzanita and Emory oak. Along this road, numerous shaded nooks provide room for movable feasts. Ever hanging overhead to the north is Milk Ranch Point, a six-square-mile mesa with a narrow causeway connecting it to the Rim. Long ago it took its name from the dairy on its top.

Looking south from a point east of Fuller Springs and the old Strawberry Grade, Coconino sandstone overhangs the village of Pine. NICK BEREZENKO

The Control Road crosses numerous live and intermittent watercourses in its 10 miles before intercepting FR 199 at the summer-home community of Whispering Pines. You can push on eastward 14 miles to where the Control Road joins State Route 260 near Kohl's Ranch on Tonto Creek. Or you can take FR 199 south, a 13-mile loop back to Payson via the Houston Mesa Road, one of the loveliest drives of the Rim country.

FR 199 visits rustic homes with shaded yards, gardens by orchards, and stone walls encircling weathered barns. It also crosses the gushing East Verde three times over concrete fords.

About two miles down FR 199, a ridge falls away to present a grand panorama of the Mazatzal Wilderness filling the horizon.

Seven and a half miles south on FR 199 to the east sprawls Sunflower Mesa and the Shoofly Village

Ruins (named for nearby Shoofly Canyon), another marker in Arizona's ancient human story. It was in Arizona that evidence placed elephant hunters as being in America more than 10,000 years ago, and Arizona excavations are pushing the time of the first Americans back to 30,000 years before present.

Not nearly that old, but no less compelling, the Shoofly Village Ruins are to the east of the Mesa del Caballo community. Archaeologists from Arizona State University investigated the ancient village during the mid-1980s.

Deriving dates from tree rings in village building timbers and from radiocarbon measurement, scientists decided that Shoofly Village was occupied as early as A.D. 1000 and peaked as an 87-house village about A.D. 1250.

These were a cosmopolitan people, perhaps at most 60 families. Forest Service archaeologists call these people the Central Arizona Tradition peoples, separate from the Salado, Mogollon, and Southern Sinagua, although perhaps they were related to the Hohokam. Over time, they built oval, masonry-lined pithouses and full rectangular houses. They grew corn, squash, and beans; hunted deer, elk, bear, and rabbit; and domesticated the dog and turkey. They fired a plain brown pottery and traded "Arizona diamonds," or quartz crystals from Diamond Point, sometimes for shell jewelry and possibly as far south as Mexico. Shoofly residents, in a most unusual project, surrounded their six-acre neighborhood with a thick, low stone wall. Although life expectancy was grimly short, the village endured — until the early 1200s, when for reasons unknown, the people throughout the region disappeared.

A wealth of data about this village emerged from the excavations, but enigmas remained. Why were village customs radically different from those in surrounding settlements? There seems to be a distinct lack of ceremonial structures, so did Shoofly residents travel elsewhere for their rituals? Give yourself a chance to ask these questions. The paved loop trail is wheelchair accessible, and the Forest Service does not charge admission. Just remember that laws forbid collecting or damaging anything. Leave nothing but footprints, take nothing but your photographs and memories.

From Payson, go north on State 87, turn right on Houston Mesa Road (FR 199), and go 1.7 miles (past Houston Mesa Campground) to a fork in the road. Stay right at the fork and go 1.2 miles to the Shoofly Village sign. The gravel drive is on the right. If you stay at the campground, the Houston Mesa Trail connects the campground to the ruins. From Shoofly, the drive to Payson is only a few miles, but . . . in history . . . it's a thousand years. ☙

W H E N   Y O U   G O . . .

Linger at the lodges and eateries, or, in the warmer season, take a trail ride with a local outfitter.

Pine/Strawberry Museum
(520) 476-3547. Open Monday through Saturday all year; closed Sunday, mid-October to mid-May. Call for hours and holiday closures.

Shoofly Village Ruins
About five miles northeast of Payson. Call Payson Ranger District, (520) 474-7900.

Tonto Natural Bridge State Park
Off State 87 about 13 miles northwest of Payson. Day use. Admission. (520) 476-4202.

Strawberry Schoolhouse
(520) 476-3095. Open weekends, mid-May through mid-October; for off-season group tours, call (520) 476-4791 or 476-3375.

Rim Country Regional Chamber of Commerce
Pine/Strawberry branch. (520) 476-3547.

Pine Canyon Trail. NICK BEREZENKO

Chapter Three

E ast of Payson four miles through the pines on State Route 260, a once-vacant ranch meadow is now an eclectic cluster of commercial enterprises. The name: Star Valley. Pat Cline holds the preeminent right to comment upon valley happenings, for in the yard of her longtime home is buried Old Man Starr (two Rs), the place's pioneer namesake. Starr died in a freighting wreck, and the Houston brothers buried him "inside the fence of the cienega so that animals couldn't walk on him." Pat (Mrs. Raymond) Cline is a third generation Haught.

One of the first generation in the Rim country, S.A. Haught once told a newspaper feature writer how he got to the Rim:

"I started out May 1, 1885, for Arizona from a point 15 miles east of Dallas City, and was driving 115 head of cattle. The Texas Panhandle had a quarantine on cattle south of the Texas and Pacific Railroad and I went through Indian Territory, thence through no man's land to New Mexico, crossed the Rio Grande River at Albuquerque, then to Holbrook and Tonto Basin. It was 450 miles out of my way . . . but I never lost a cow."

CIRCUM-NAVIGATING
Diamond Point

It says something about the tenacity of the Haught strain that, more than a hundred years later, S.A. had three sons living — one sired when S.A. was in his 70s.

When Pat was young, today's State 260 through Star Valley was just a gravel road barely wagon wide with occasional turnouts for passing. Things change. Not long ago, while working as a highway construction flag woman, Pat stood with arms akimbo and shook her head at something big going on.

"Civilization has arrived," she said, "when they put concrete sidewalks along the road through Star Valley."

(LEFT) This young bull is one of a burgeoning population of Rocky Mountain elk. This species was transplanted long ago from Yellowstone to take the place of extinct Merriam's elk. WILLIAM E. BARCUS
(RIGHT) Pat and Raymond Cline show off a pair of family branding irons at their older-than-a-century homesite in Star Valley. NICK BEREZENKO

It is true. In a monumental work, State Route 260 below the Rim has become more freeway than lane; the main artery of the Rim country speeds travelers across the northern portion of the land below the Rim. Trips that used to take days now can be done in minutes.

All that said, you have to wonder what those folks three and four generations ago would make of Star Valley and its sidewalks now, and of the businesses that have sprouted nearby.

Local resident Marvin Isbell owned one of those businesses — the BZB Nursery — before it closed, and he still probably knows more than anybody about gardening the Southwest between 5,000 and 6,000 feet — a broad contour of problem soils, killer winds, insect plagues, and two months (May and June) that often can go straight through with

droop with limbloads of luscious bounty. Those Southwestern standbys — corn, squash, beans — bolt past July into September; they grew in the Rim country thousands of years before Columbus. Other consistent winners are green onions, string beans, tomatoes, peppers, and berries.

Roses love warm seasons in the Rim country, but require winter protection. Long ago, some pioneer brought a darkly hued domestic iris bulb and today it is everywhere, nicknamed Payson Purple. Here's a little list of other flowers that do well in the Rim's realm: cosmos, zinnias, hollyhocks, and forsythia.

Call it human nature, but perhaps it is through plants and animals that we relate to a national forest. The primary tree associated with the Rim country is the ponderosa pine. It rises up out of the ground, gestures grandly, and tosses its hair. It pro-

scarcely a drop of rain. The Rim country also can experience a mild winter, a balmy, moist spring, an idyllic summer, and an autumn that pours a cornucopia of vegetables and fruit into Rim kitchens and roadside produce stands.

But don't count on it.

"Just when you think you have it figured out," says Isbell, "January comes in April, and August extends into October. Or the grasshoppers explode, or the javelinas raid, or the elk dismantle the elk-proof fences. It helps to keep in mind that even in the mountains we're still within a semi-arid state. Spells of low humidity are as much to be feared as late and early frosts."

So much for accentuating the negative. Orchards of apples and peaches and apricots some years

vides oxygen, shade, food, shelter, habitat, even music. Yes, as John Muir declared of the ponderosa, "Of all pines, this one gives forth the finest music to the winds."

Photographer and author Jim Tallon adds: "More than a thousand species of wildlife are interrelated with — and, in some cases, dependent upon — the ponderosa pine."

For a trip through this ponderosa pine forest and more, you're offered a loop that takes State Route 260 from Payson, past Star Valley to the east end of the Control Road, then circles back west and south for a return to Payson. Often in view out the left-hand window looms 6,384-foot Diamond Point, a minor but strategically located rise from which much fire-endangered forest can be scanned for tell-tale smoke. Diamond Point got its name from fields of quartz crystals that litter the area.

It was from Forest Service Road 64, 15.2 miles east of Payson, that the defense was mounted

(ABOVE) An aerial tanker zooms in to drop fire-retardant slurry onto the Dude Fire, June, 1990. NICK BEREZENKO
(OPPOSITE PAGE, LEFT TO RIGHT) Wild iris, Indian paintbrush, columbine, and wild Arizona rose — the colors of Rim country gardens. STEWART AITCHISON
(OPPOSITE PAGE, BELOW) His green thumb reaching to the elbow, Marvin Isbell pinches back tea roses . NICK BEREZENKO

against one of the worst fires in Arizona's history. The Control Road passes through several burned-over miles and affords access to the Dude Fire Auto Tour. On the way, the road passes clusters of summer homes and crosses several trout streams, such as Bonita and Ellison creeks, the latter named for the father of Miss Duette Ellison.

The Ellisons founded the Apple Ranch with its 3,000 fruit trees. Located as it was on a main east-west trail, the Apple Ranch served as a way station for travelers through the 1880s and '90s. Miss Duette, a vivacious and musically talented ranch girl, married governor-to-be George W.P. Hunt to become Arizona's *first* First Lady.

But regarding the Dude Fire. On a dry, windy day in late June, 1990, lightning ignited a fire in the Dude Creek drainage 12 miles northeast of Payson. For a week the conflagration roared across the face of the Rim, eventually costing the lives of six firefighters, blackening 24,174 acres, destroying

51 cabins, chasing a thousand people from their homes, and doing $12 million in damage. The holocaust took out a swath three miles wide and 14 miles long, and, by insidious selection, burned down Zane Grey's cabin and the equally historic Babe Haught log house nearby.

The FR 29 turnoff to the Dude Fire Auto Tour is 4.2 miles west of State Route 260. (The Payson Ranger Station offers a free informative brochure "The Story of the Dude Burn.") As you drive the tour, you come upon the numbered posts, pointing out the fire's devastation:

Post 1. This is what the forest looked like before the burn.

Post 2. The Rim dead ahead, so huge it can create its own weather.

Post 3. A place where the fire was fought with bulldozed fire lines and aerial bombardment with chemical retardant.

Post 4. A badly burned place, reseeded with soil-holding plants.

Post 5. Thoroughly charred, it will be generations before the forest returns. But much is sprouting.

Post 6. Same fire, different results. On one side of the road the fire burned incredibly hot, actually boiling and exploding sap. Across the road the fire took away ground fuel, and left many trees untouched.

The relatively unpopulated grandeur of Tonto National Forest, as seen from Diamond Point, southward over Star Valley to the distant Mazatzal Wilderness. NICK BEREZENKO

Post 7. An erosion control structure.

Post 8. Only blackened sticks remain.

Post 9. Lushly growing ground cover, some from the 250,000 pounds of seed broadcast via helicopters immediately after the fire.

Post 10. Private land, where luckily no homes were destroyed.

Posts 11 and 12 can be reached only by high-clearance vehicles, preferably with four-wheel drive. Post 11 marks the old Roberts Burn of 1961, which is returning to forest. Post 12 is at Big Canyon, where nature is healing itself after severe erosion. In all, the motoring tour extends seven miles.

"It's like springtime every day out there," observed a Payson ranger. He explained that before occupation by whites, the forest burned periodically — set afire by lightning or the Indians. Because of the fires' frequency, fuel for hot disastrous blazes did not accumulate. A century of unnatural fire suppression allowed forest debris to pile up and carry fire into treetops.

Now, the Dude Burn area experiences its own renewal. With the help of its friends, long-range programs of reforestation, stream protection, fisheries revival, trail stabilization, and wildlife assistance are progressing. In time, this blackened portion of the Tonto National Forest will be more gorgeous than before the Dude Fire.

Back on the Control Road, just a tenth of a mile past FR 29, FR 65 leads you four miles to Diamond Point Lookout. The views from the point are sensational, and in summer, you'll find other visitors to Diamond Point — swarms of colorful ladybugs.

From the Dude tour, the Control Road progresses through ancient alligator juniper, dry washes, and green forest for 4.5 miles, to enter the southern portion of the Dude Burn. Then for nearly three miles you drive through gradually mending burnscape. Two miles more and you join FR 199. Turn south to return 13 miles to Payson. And ever on your left looms the landmark Diamond Point. ◼

W H E N   Y O U   G O . . .

This part of the Rim country lies in the Tonto National Forest's Payson Ranger District. The ranger station is at 1009 East Highway 260, Payson, (520) 474-7900. If you plan to hike the area, ask about topography ("topo") maps here. Other maps, brochures, and chummy advice are readily available.

Some of that advice would be to always pack along enough water (a minimum of a gallon per person per day), since stream flow can't be counted on. Stay current with the weather reports; Rim country weather can change suddenly. Follow all fire restrictions, especially when forest fire danger is high.

If you're not in the hiking mood but prefer a tough view of Territorial ranching life along the Rim, read the classic novel *Filaree* (University of New Mexico Press: Albuquerque, 1998 edition). Author Marguerite Noble, a longtime Payson resident, based the authentic tale on her mother's life.

Hard to believe this placid trickle of Tonto Creek at the Bear Flat crossing can be transformed into a torrent when the heavens open over the Mogollon. NICK BEREZENKO

DON'T EVEN THINK ABOUT DOING IT

One March, a warm rain fell on the snow pack. Of a late morning we inched our way down the slippery, eroded road to Bear Flat. We wanted to watch Tonto Creek roll boulders and toss tree trunks. We were not disappointed. The normally placid ford over to the summer homes was transformed into a violent sluice. Presently, a most improbable figure appeared on the eastern shore: a young man covered by mud.

"I need a pull," he cried.

Well, you'd almost have to own a four-wheeler to understand how difficult it can be to turn down a sincere plea for a rescue. It's sort of a priestly calling.

I had been across the ford dozens of times, and I thought I knew the bottom. So with little dawdling, I launched my hoopie into the maelstrom. Deeper than I thought! And whoops! in midstream the bottom was gone — all the way to Hells Gate, likely. Then the engine upped and died.

Tonto heaved its strength against the left side of the little Jeep, which now and then would give a bit of ground toward the churning rapids downstream. It dawned on me that I was either going to save my life by saving the Jeep or probably lose them both.

Yes, luck. In the back were a couple of dry rags and a toolbox. I fetched a wrench, climbed out around the windshield, stood on a flat fender, and threw back the hood. Water propelled by the radiator fan had drenched the spark plugs and distributor. I dried them the best I could. The Jeep jumped downstream a couple of feet. Quickly, I reached underwater, loosened the generator bracket with the wrench, and removed the fan belt from the pulley.

Flopped the hood shut. Swung around the windshield. Hit the ignition. Vaaaaa-roooom! Jeep and I roared out of the water pocket and made the other side.

In the recklessness of youth, I pulled the fellow's sedan out of a bog, dropped my tow bar onto his trailer hitch, removed his fan belt, and plunged into Tonto Creek a second time. We aimed in tandem as high upstream as physics allowed, and we emerged within inches of missing the downstream exit. We clawed to safety like a mechanical alligator.

Then we opened some drinks and laughed so long and hard that the tears streaked from our faces and splashed onto trembling hands.

If not too low-slung, most cars in good condition can make it to Tonto Creek if FR 405 isn't wet or cut by rain. FR 405 leaves the south side of State Route 260 at the Thompson Draw Summer Homes Unit I turnoff, 14.4 miles east of Payson. To Bear Flat is about seven miles, and the last four-mile stretch is a pistol: 24 percent grades, washboard surface, and throat-grabbing overviews. You must take the outer lane descending, but soothe your nerves in the knowledge that you get the inner lane returning.

At the flat is a small but handsome camping area, a massive concrete apron, and access to favorite stocked fishing holes. Even with the newer apron, I would not launch an atomic submarine into the flooded Tonto, let alone a car. That applies to you, too. Don't even *think* about doing it! ⛰

COCONINO NATIONAL FOREST

West Clear Creek

FR 81

FR 81E

FR 211

FH 3

To Flagstaff

87 To Winslow

Blue Ridge Ranger Station

FR 138

Clints Well Campground

Clints Well

Blue Ridge Campground

FR 751

Rock Crossing Campground

FR 95

Blue Ridge Reservoir

Coconino Nat. For.

Apache-Sitgreaves Nat. For.

WEST CLEAR CREEK WILDERNESS

Calloway Lake

East Clear Creek

Battleground Ridge Fight FR 123E

FR 123

To Camp Verde

260

General Crook Trail

87

FR 147

FR 141

Crackerbox Canyon

FR 95

Pinchot Springs Cabin

Barbershop Canyon

FR 96

MOGOLLON PLATEAU

Kehl Campground

General Springs Cabin

Battle of Big Dry Wash Monument

FR 137

Buck Springs Cabin

Knoll Lake Campground

FOSSIL SPRINGS WILDERNESS

FR 300

Baker Butte

FR 218A

Pine Canyon Trail

Milk Ranch Point

FR 218

Washington Park

Gila County

Coconino County

FR 300

FR 295E

Knoll Lake

87

Highline Trail

FR 199

FR 32

Verde Glen

Highline Trail

Bear Canyon Lake

Strawberry Schoolhouse

FR 708

STRAWBERRY

Strawberry Valley

PINE

Donahue Trail

Highline Trail

FR 64

Third Crossing

Second Crossing

Water Wheel

Ellison

First Crossing

Creek

FR 64

Zane Grey Lodge site

Myrtle Point

Fish Hatchery

FR 300

Highline Trail

FR 289

Promontory Butte

Upper Tonto Creek Campground

Kohl's Ranch

FR 428

Oak Springs Trail

FR 64

River

Webber Creek

Tonto Creek Campground

Tonto Village

260

Chris

TONTO NATIONAL FOREST

FR 583

FR 65

FR 64

Camp Tontozona

FR 405

Bear Flat

Christophe Creek Campground

Tonto Natural Bridge State Park

FR 272

Flowing Spring

FR 622

Diamond Rim

Ponderosa Campground

MAZATZAL WILDERNESS

Verde

East

87

Houston Mesa

Diamond Point Lookout

260

Payson Airport

PAYSON

Star Valley

Payson Ranger Station

FR 406

Pine Creek

HELLSGATE WILDERNESS

Tonto Creek

Mazatzal Mtns.

Tonto Apache Ind. Res.

To Phoenix

The Mogollon Rim Country, land for all seasons: In spring canoes cruise the clear waters of Rim lakes.

Summer brings hikes along the gurgling streams that flow from beneath The Rim.

PHOTOS BY NICK BEREZENKO

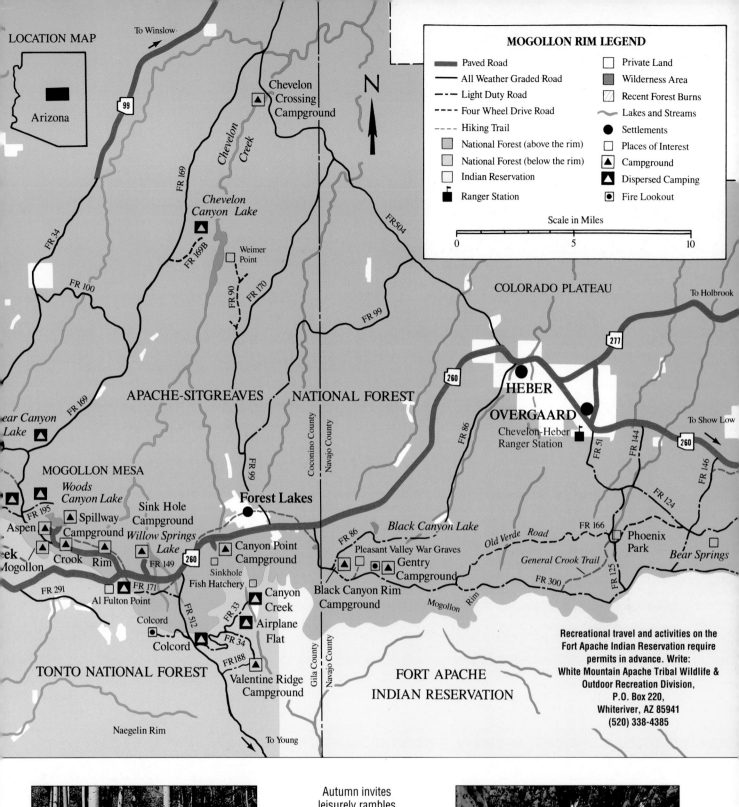

LOCATION MAP

Arizona

To Winslow

MOGOLLON RIM LEGEND

Paved Road
All Weather Graded Road
Light Duty Road
Four Wheel Drive Road
Hiking Trail
National Forest (above the rim)
National Forest (below the rim)
Indian Reservation
Ranger Station

Private Land
Wilderness Area
Recent Forest Burns
Lakes and Streams
Settlements
Places of Interest
Campground
Dispersed Camping
Fire Lookout

Scale in Miles

0   5   10

Chevelon
Crossing
Campground

Chevelon Creek

FR 169

Chevelon Canyon Lake

FR 169B

Weimer Point

FR 90

FR 170

FR 504

FR 99

COLORADO PLATEAU

To Holbrook

277

260

HEBER

FR 86

OVERGAARD

Chevelon-Heber
Ranger Station

To Show Low

FR 51

FR 144

260

FR 146

FR 34

FR 100

APACHE-SITGREAVES   NATIONAL FOREST

FR 169

FR 99

Coconino County

Navajo County

FR 124

Bear Canyon Lake

MOGOLLON MESA

Woods Canyon Lake

FR 195

Spillway

Aspen

Campground

Willow Springs Lake

Crook

Rim

FR 149

Mogollon

260

Forest Lakes

Sink Hole
Campground

Canyon Point
Campground

Sinkhole
Fish Hatchery

FR 86

Black Canyon Lake

Pleasant Valley War Graves

Gentry
Campground

Black Canyon Rim
Campground

Old Verde Road

FR 166

General Crook Trail

Phoenix
Park

Bear Springs

FR 125

FR 291

Al Fulton Point

FR 171

Canyon
Creek

Airplane
Flat

Mogollon Rim

FR 300

Colcord

FR 512

FR 33

Colcord

FR 34

FR 188

Valentine Ridge
Campground

Gila County

Navajo County

**FORT APACHE
INDIAN RESERVATION**

TONTO NATIONAL FOREST

Naegelin Rim

To Young

Recreational travel and activities on the
Fort Apache Indian Reservation require
permits in advance. Write:
White Mountain Apache Tribal Wildlife &
Outdoor Recreation Division,
P.O. Box 220,
Whiteriver, AZ 85941
(520) 338-4385

Autumn invites
leisurely rambles
among the quaking
aspens.
JAMES TALLON

Winter beckons the
cross-country skier to
explore the pristine
countryside.
BRIAN BECK

Chapter Four

Tonto Creek

WHERE LIFE QUICKENS

Kohl's Ranch, perched on the west bank of Tonto Creek, is not so much a ranch as a village complete with a lovely hotel, restaurant, and summer homes. Kohl's put up guests free when it was a cow ranch in the 1880s, then new owners began charging for bed and board in 1927. As late as the 1950s, a tiny tavern boasted of seven stools and one curvaceous Coca-Cola glass for "If," as the aromatic, grizzly, toothless bartender was fond of saying, "a lady ever stops by, but so far, she hain't."

Women were so scarce for all-night dances, men had to dance with brooms while waiting for the chance to cut in. Now, lots of ladies stop by.

In addition to the fishing, camping, hunting, horseback riding, and hosting in and around Kohl's, across the creek beckons the Open Air Chapel where local pastors conduct nondenominational services on summerish Sabbaths.

Down the Tonto from Kohl's sprawls Camp Tontozona. Here, during training dates in late summer, visitors are welcome to witness the football geniuses of Arizona State University whip young Sun Devils into shape. Large public campgrounds bracket Kohl's

Ranch, with some campsites big enough for trailers and motor homes.

There used to be two outstanding destinations in the Kohl's Ranch area. Now one is gone. On June 27, 1990, the Dude Fire destroyed the cabin where Zane Grey chose to spend much of his time in the early 20th century. Where he wrote Western novels, often in 30 days of intense scribbling. Where he based his hunts after bear, lion, and deer. And where in 1929 he brought a group of friends and planned a big hunting party out of season. Arizona would not allow it, and Grey threw a fit. Arizona owed him for the publicity he brought to it, he fumed. Grey vowed to leave the state forever . . . and did.

(OPPOSITE PAGE) Deciduous trees such as black walnut, oak, and box elder commingle with conifers along Tonto Creek near Kohl's Ranch. By summer's end, wild grapevines drape trees as high as 40 feet.
JERRY JACKA
(RIGHT) Before slipping it back into the water, a young fisherwoman shows off her Tonto Creek crayfish.
NICK BEREZENKO

For three decades, the cabin deteriorated until it caught the attention of Phoenix air-conditioning magnate William Goettl (rhymes with metal). Goettl purchased the property from the Grey family in 1962, and he and his crew restored the cabin to its original status. It was opened for the enjoyment and education of the public and, in 1974, was included in the National Register of Historic Places.

On a happier note, the state's Tonto Creek Fish Hatchery was saved by a brave and determined crew of firefighters in the same day that the adjacent Grey cabin burned.

That hatchery holds a special, sentimental place in my psyche as one of my first trout-fishing treks 40 years ago:

The ex-World War II Jeep in four-wheel drive slogs through the frost-heaved decomposed granite of the steeply pitched forest path, climbing from an elevation of 5,600 to 6,400 feet in a reach of about four miles.

The thin, conifer-perfumed late-March air pours through the tiny, doorless 4X4 and pierces my quilted parka. Patches of snow blanket the north-facing slopes. Along the way, I am startled by a herd of pregnant mule deer does and delighted by gray squirrels busily trying to recall where they cached their acorns from last fall.

At last I can see a rustic gate, which I take to be the end of the trail. The heavy snow pack under and beyond the Rim has not yet melted, but Tonto Creek is running a fair head of water. With numbed fingers, I fiddle with rod and reel, line and leader. . . .

Fluffy, moist snowflakes begin to flutter down through the hardwoods, almost making me decide to hike my cold feet to the Jeep and retreat. But in a short walk upstream, I come to a fence beyond which lurks a huge, quiet, bramble-free pool. The fence is not much of a barrier — just a few strands of wire through which a bull elk might amble.

There, even an amateur fly-caster should luck out. And that I do. On the first presentation of an artificial larva, the pond's surface erupts with a primeval

(ABOVE, LEFT) Campfire and lantern illuminate a cozy bivouac at Christopher Creek Campground. Nearby rises Christopher Mountain, a dandy expanse for hunting during deer season. NICK BEREZENKO (ABOVE, RIGHT) Cabins, cafes, and other roadside facilities, including RV and mobile home parks, come together at Christopher Creek, five miles east of Kohl's Ranch on State Route 260. NICK BEREZENKO (OPPOSITE PAGE) Somewhere near serene Christopher Creek, legend goes, is buried the fortune of the first local settler, Isadore Christopher. P.K. WEIS

force. Then the fish feels the hook and sounds. The line seems anchored to the bottom. I sense a bit of give, gain a few feet, and gently play the lunker near to the shore.

With a swish of my net, the great rainbow, fat with roe, maybe 15, 16 inches long, is mine. With every cast, there rises another monster trout.

When I am done, I dismantle my gear and pack the fish into my creel. They overfill it, and I must tote a few on a string.

Then I notice a humble road lying a few hundred feet to the west. Why fight my way through the thickets? I climb onto a piece of meadow and stroll down the road toward the Jeep. At the gate is posted a

hand-crafted sign: "Hope you enjoyed your visit to the Tonto Creek Fish Hatchery."

I have been fishing in a brood pond!

I skulk back into the woods, stow the gear and plunder in my get-away vehicle, smear some mud on my license plate, and light a shuck for home.

Thank the Lord for statutes of limitations. Even I am welcome back at the scene of my crime, and you, too, if you leave your fishing gear in your car.

The hatchery is open seven days a week, 8 A.M. to 4 P.M., all year. Self-guided tours and a visitor center will inform you that while a natural trout stream can produce only about 225 catchable fish per mile, each year, the Tonto hatchery produces 180,000 in the same period. From egg to nine-incher takes about a year. About 2,500 fish are distributed into Tonto, Christopher, and Verde drainages on a normal weekend. The stocking is doubled for holidays.

"The source of Tonto Creek is itself a special phenomenon," writes my friend George Collins. "It flows at the rate of 1,500 gallons per minute; the headwaters maintain a constant temperature of 48 degrees. Established in 1936, the hatchery is an absorbingly interesting place, educational and useful, worth far more than it costs."

It's sad to leave such havens. But more places of interest, such as Christopher Creek, summon you on. Local chronicler Peggy Benz offers a bit of history:

"Christopher Creek [the community] is located just 25 miles northeast of Payson on Highway 260 at an elevation of 6,000 feet. Both Christopher Creek and Christopher Mountain were named in honor of an early French settler Isador Christopher. . . . He lived here with his mail-order bride, Mary. In July 1882, Christopher had killed a bear, skinned it, and hung the skinned bear in one of his cabins. While he was out hunting the next day, Apaches came and burned two of his buildings. And while these buildings were still smoldering, U.S. Army troops came along. They found these animal remains and,

(LEFT) Mature rainbow trout cruise a holding pond at Tonto Creek Fish Hatchery. The hatchery can produce annually a quarter million fish and two million fingerlings for stocking Arizona waters. BOB AND SUZANNE CLEMENZ
(OPPOSITE PAGE, TOP) U.S. cavalrymen inter the incinerated remains of a skinned bear, believing it was Old Man Christopher's corpse. SCRATCH BOARD ILLUSTRATION BY BILL AHRENDT

thinking the Indians had killed Christopher, the troops gave the bear a solemn funeral and burial."

After frisking in the fresh air, don't let that grisly tale affect your appetite when several good restaurants prosper at Christopher Creek. The Christopher Creek area also has large public campgrounds, dependable fishing, and a wonder-filled network of hiking and horse trails.

Then snug down your seat belts. The nine-mile piece of State Route 260 from Christopher Creek to the top of the Mogollon Rim is a marvelous but contentious marriage between road engineers and Mother Nature. With Promontory Butte and like land masses darkening the north, the modern tarmac bends and climbs past the 260 Trailhead (eastern terminus of the Highline Trail) and at times soars heavenward so sharply your car will seem like a

flying machine in takeoff. Looking southward, you'll see four, five, six, seven blue-gray ridges come into view, and by the time you reach the top at Al Fulton Point, the feeling of flight almost becomes real. It's as though you are floating above a painting by Maynard Dixon or Ed Mell.

You could find no better spot for contemplating nature. It calls to mind the musings of such early American naturalists as Henry David Thoreau: "This curious world we inhabit is more wonderful than convenient; more beautiful than it is useful; it is more to be admired and enjoyed than used."; and John Muir: "Climb the mountains and get their good tidings. Nature's peace will flow into you as sunshine flows into trees. The winds will blow their own freshness into you and the storms their energy, while cares will drop off like autumn leaves." ◆

WHEN YOU GO...

Facilities here under the Rim are concentrated on old homestead land like Star Valley, Kohl's Ranch, and Christopher Creek. You can find food, fuel, and lodgings at all three.

Managed by the Arizona Game and Fish Department, the Tonto Creek Fish Hatchery is at the end of FR 289, four miles north from State Route 260, (520) 478-4200. Enjoy the hatchery's popular self-guided tour seven days a week (except Thanksgiving and Christmas days), 8 A.M. to 4 P.M. No charge.

Obtain more outdoor recreation information and brochures from the Forest Service's district offices in Payson, Tonto National Forest, (520) 474-7900, and in Overgaard, Apache-Sitgreaves National Forests, (520) 535-4481.

Many stables under and atop the Mogollon Rim rent saddle horses for exploring backcountry tracks dating to frontier times. This trio rides along the Highline Trail near Horton Creek.
NICK BEREZENKO

IN QUEST OF THE GHOST OF HORTON CREEK

When you hike up Horton Creek, you enter an Eden tragically lost by an Arizona pioneer.

Fittingly, Horton Creek today is somewhat invisible — and that fact tends to keep away the crowds that congregate nearby. On weekends, only a few find the delights of Horton, and on weekdays, a hiker might have the hidden haven all alone. And nowhere will the modern walker join the company of a more kindred spirit from a century ago.

As a teenage boy, L.J. Horton with his sickly dad walked all the way from his home in Michigan to the promised land of California in 1863. By 1881, Horton, now married and 33 years old, drifted into Arizona to establish a freighting business. As early as 1882 he located a ranch 20 miles to the east of Payson, on a tributary of Tonto Creek. In the copious manuscripts Horton later left to posterity, he described a lush refuge of grapevines and black walnuts, acres of wild iris and fields of native vegetables, a land flowing with milk and free honey — and unflagging neighbors.

By 1887, Horton "was milking 31 head of cows. I had not sold a steer or cow. I had kept all of my five years' increase. My freighting business paid all the expenses." He took an inventory and counted 211 head of beef cattle on his range. Then for a few months he had to journey south.

"I returned early in the spring . . . 1888, heavily loaded with supplies. My trail wagon was loaded with fruit trees and shrubbery to beautify my place. All looked the same except that I saw no cattle. Neither did I see any signs of cattle around the salt lick. . . . I rode and searched the range for three months and failed to discover any cattle or any evidence. In July I gave my shrubbery to a neighbor.

"Once more in my life, like the blowing of a leaf, I am cast back with only the blind future to guide me. I never in all my wanderings had found a place that I learned to love so well."

Rustlers not only stole the cattle, but they effectively robbed Horton of the ability to make a living as a rancher. He was forced to abandon his claim and go back to freighting.

In frontiersman Horton's time, his creek flowed above ground to spill into Tonto. But early in this century, the creek apparently cut its way through limestone to disappear into caverns which likely feed springs along the bigger Tonto Creek. So the first half-mile of hiking is past what appears to be an unpromising and barren dry wash.

But once you reach the water, you'll encounter verdant creekside vegetation and picture postcard waterfalls. Exactly where Horton built his cabin and corrals is unknown, but several meadows with rock ruins are possibilities.

This trail (#285) offers options — an easy stroll up an old road above the creek, or a moderate hike along the creekside path, both ending at the springs where the creek originates. You also have the option of returning the way you came or hiking west (on the Highline Trail #31) to the junction of the Highline and the Hatchery Trail, 100 yards south of Tonto Fish Hatchery Road, FR 289. Whatever your choice, when you emerge from your journey to Horton's lost homestead, you'll fully appreciate a footnote he scribbled on his manuscript:

"In 1891 I got a letter from Mr. [Jesse] Ellison saying, 'Horton, I do not believe you have any cattle here. I herewith enclose eight dollars for one old cow.'

"That was all I got out of that five years' struggle." ✍

Horton Creek
Trail Information

DIFFICULTY: Easy to moderate.

TRAIL ACCESS: Drive east from Payson on State Route 260 just past Kohl's Ranch, turn left on FR 289, and go one mile to Upper Tonto Creek Campground. For the upper trailhead, continue on FR 289 about 2.5 miles to the end of the pavement at the Fish Hatchery Road. There the Hatchery Trail leads 100 yards to the south and connects with the Highline Trail heading east to Horton Springs.

ELEVATION: 5,300 - 6,700 feet.

DISTANCE: Four miles one way to the springs. Distance from the springs to the hatchery is 3.4 miles.

HIKING TIME: Two to three hours one way.

SEASON: April-November.

MARKED: Oak trail signs and tree blazes.

WATER: Horton Creek and Horton Springs. Treat all water.

PARKING: Horton Trail — lot at Horton Picnic Ground across from Upper Tonto Campground. Hatchery Trail — Roadside at end of pavement (Fish Hatchery Road) at the Hatchery trailhead.

CONTACT: Payson Ranger District, (520) 474-7900.

(OPPOSITE PAGE) Nature provides a bridge at Horton Springs, just under the face of the Rim.
(BELOW) Moss-covered granite boulders, lush grass, beds of watercress, and piney bowers beautify the grotto where Horton Creek rises at Horton Springs.
PHOTOS BY NICK BEREZENKO

RIM CAMPING

I t's hard to imagine anything in a lifetime that has changed so radically as how so many Americans camp. Two generations ago, camping was primitive by comparison, with gear lashed to running boards and food preserved in cans. The highest tech marvel was a Coleman lantern.

Now in the nation a million campgrounds as often as not boast electricity, water, and sewer hookups. Getting away from it all no longer is the game for many Americans. Clearly, they want to get closer to nature, but at the same time take the rough out of roughing it. Psychologists say the new breed of camper is a child of the urban shift, uncomfortable and lonesome in too much space.

In a twist of irony, foresters consider the RV revolution to be the salvation of our woodlands. Their users do far less damage to the environment than those bygone bivouackers who chopped wood, fed warming and cooking fires, and buried garbage which animals promptly exhumed and scattered.

Yet the sheer numbers of people visiting Arizona's wooded refuges today are so multiplied that even considerate, contained, ethical camping is putting the land at risk.

Alarmed foresters and representatives set into motion the Arizona Recreation Initiative, now pumping funds into dozens of Forest Service projects and partnerships. The hope is that the new facilities will

Campgrounds

SITE NAME	APPROX. ELEV.	SEASONS OF USE	DAYS' LIMIT	FEE	NO. OF UNITS	SAFE WATER	REST ROOMS	RV LENGTH LIMIT (FT.)	WASTE DISP.	TABLE/ BENCH/ FIRE RING	BOATING NEARBY	FISHING NEARBY
ASPEN	7,500	MAY-OCT.	14	X	136	X	X	32	X	X	X	X
BLACK CANYON RIM	7,600	MAY-OCT.	14	X	21	X	X	16	X	X		
BLUE RIDGE	7,300	MAY-SEPT.	14	X	10	X	X	32		X		
CANYON POINT	7,600	MAY-OCT.	14	X	117	X	X	75	X	X		
CHEVELON CROSSING	6,300	MAR.-DEC.	14		7		X	16		X		X
CHRISTOPHER CREEK	5,600	MAY-OCT.	14	X	43	X	X	22		X		X
CLINTS WELL	7,000	APR.-NOV.	14		12		X	22		X		
CROOK	7,600	MAY-OCT.	14	X	26	X	X	32	X	X	X	X
GENTRY	7,700	MAY-NOV.	14		6		X	16		X		
HOUSTON MESA	5,000	ALL YEAR	14	X	105	X	X	30	X	X		
KEHL SPRINGS	7,500	MAY-SEPT.	14		8		X	22		X		
KNOLL LAKE	7,500	MAY-SEPT.	14	X	33	X	X	32		X	X	X
MOGOLLON	7,600	MAY-OCT.	14	X	26	X	X	32	X	X		
PONDEROSA	5,600	ALL YEAR	14	X	61	X	X	22	X	X		
RIM	7,500	MAY-SEPT.	14	X	26	X	X	32	X	X		X
ROCK CROSSING	7,500	MAY-SEPT.	14	X	35	X	X	32		X	X	X
SINKHOLE	7,500	MAY-OCT.	14	X	26	X	X	32	X	X	X	X
SPILLWAY	7,500	MAY-SEPT.	14	X	26	X	X	16	X	X	X	X
LOWER/UPPER TONTO CREEK	5,500	APRIL-NOV.	14	X	17/9	X	X	22		X		X
VALENTINE RIDGE	6,600	APRIL-NOV.	14		9		X	16		X		

catch up with demand, and thereafter reasonable sums will keep the places and programs maintained and going.

But even if all this comes to pass, *you* are the key to success. Plan ahead. Honor signs. Stay on trails. Don't trench around tents. Kill fires. Follow sensible sanitation rules. Don't wash dishes or clean fish in lakes and streams. And regarding litter: Pack it in, and pack it out. Take from nature nothing but memories; leave nothing but footprints.

Then maybe the lyrical thought of John Muir will thrive into perpetuity: "I used to envy the father of our race, dwelling as he did in contact with the new-made fields and plants of Eden; but I do so no more, because I have discovered that I also live in creation's dawn. The morning stars still sing together, and the world, not yet half made, becomes more beautiful every day." ◼

Dispersed Camping Areas*

SITE NAME		APPROX. ELEV.	SEASONS OF USE	DAYS' LIMIT	NO. OF UNITS	REST ROOMS	RV LENGTH LIMIT (FT.)	BOATING	FISHING
AIRPLANE FLAT		6,600	APRIL-NOV.	14		X	16		X
BEAR CANYON LAKE		7,600	APRIL-OCT.	14		X	22	X	X
UPPER CANYON CREEK		6,600	APRIL-NOV.	14		X	16		X
CHEVELON CANYON LAKE		6,900	MARCH-DEC.	14		X	16	X	X
COLCORD RIDGE		7,600	APRIL-NOV.	14		X	32		
EAST VERDE COMPLEX	FLOWING SPG (FR 272)	4,600	MAY-SEPT.	14			16		X
	WATER WHEEL (FR 199)	5,000	MAY-SEPT.	14			16		X
	2ND X-ING (FR 199)	5,100	MAY-SEPT.	14			16		X
	3RD X-ING (FR 199)	5,100	MAY-SEPT.	14			16		X
	VERDE GLEN (FR 199)	5,600	MAY-SEPT.	14			16		X
FR 9350		7,600	MAY-SEPT.	14	42				
FR 195		7,600	MAY-SEPT.	14	20				
AL FULTON PT (FR 171)		7,600	APRIL-OCT.	14	50				
FR 169		7,700	APRIL-OCT.	14	5				

(ABOVE) A couple of America's 8.5 million recreation vehicles tarry a spell at the Forest Service's Aspen Campground near Woods Canyon Lake. It's estimated that nearly a million citizens a year now visit the Rim country. Nick Berezenko

Almost all Rim country campgrounds are first come, first served. However, you may make reservations at Aspen, Canyon Point, Christopher Creek, Ponderosa, and Spillway campgrounds. Reservations are required at Houston Mesa.

Call toll-free 1-877-444-6777. Campground reservations require 10 days' notice. You may pay the fee with credit card or check, but once you hang up the phone, the transaction is final.

* **Dispersed Camping Areas** have few facilities, no drinking water, and no fee. All camping must be self-contained. Go the extra mile – pack out more than you pack in.

Chapter Five

East Atop The Rim

HIGH, WIDE, AND WILD

Following your breath-stopping ascension to the top of the Rim, there opens a plateau of park-like woods, shallow lakes, rolling undulations, pancake-flat cienegas, sinkholes, limestone ledges, and tentative little drainages.

Some spritzes of water leap off the Rim southward as intermittent waterfalls, but most water sources follow a gentler pull of gravity northward, eventually gathering to slice deep canyons bisecting the tablelands. Clear and Chevelon creeks, for example, spill topside runoff into the Little Colorado River. And rain and snowmelt ultimately may race northwestward another hundred miles before ramming west through the gut of Grand Canyon and on down the Colorado River.

On top, at Al Fulton Point, the altimeter reads 7,600 feet, and you feel a sharper bite in the wind and sense a thinness of air. Forester Tim Grier knows the story about Al Fulton Point. He says Al and brother Harry dared to drive a herd of sheep through cattle range, and cowman Wilford Scarlett stampeded the flock toward a sinkhole. Poor Al fell in and died.

Says Tim: "The original headstone, now missing, read, 'Murdered in 1888,' *not* 'Shot in 1901' as the tombstone now reads."

Tim recommends an easy, brief hike that rather typifies the relaxed lay of the land on the backside of the Rim. Signs lead away, along the General Crook Trail, from the southeast corner of the Al Fulton Point parking lot. The trail progresses 2,200 feet to a small sign pointing the way another 600 feet to Al's grave. It's an easy walk, about a mile round trip. It's usually pleasant, April through November, and the parking lot overviews will leave you bug-eyed.

State Route 260 from Fulton to Heber narrows to two lanes, but the 22 miles sail across as pretty a highland as Arizona has to offer.

About three miles east of Fulton Point, the Young Road,

(OPPOSITE PAGE) Fir, pine, and oak form an almost unbroken mantle from Al Fulton Point to the distant Mazatzals. During the summer, national forest staffers at Fulton Point's log-cabin visitors center share information for the entire Rim area.
WESLEY HOLDEN
(RIGHT) Al Fulton's grave has a humble, handmade headstone, but it's near a million-dollar view. NICK BEREZENKO

FR 512, goes south three miles to FR 33 which eases eastward to secluded Canyon Creek. Here the state operates another fish hatchery (open for tours), and this stream is limited to artificial fly and lure fishing only. Canyon Creek was one of the first creeks set aside so that purist fly-casters should not have to compete side by side with more numerous bait anglers. A number of fly fishers go another step: using barbless hooks so that after the battle their catch may be easily released unharmed.

Back on State Route 260, as you proceed eastward, you come to Forest Lakes, a sylvan community in and around the historic Long Tom spread. Forest Lakes holds a number of year-round residents as well as summer people. There's a restaurant, lodge, gas station, small grocery, and, in winter, cross-country skiing is in vogue. Forest Lakes Touring Center rents skis and grooms trails; when the snow vanishes, the action turns to canoeing and other sports.

Another cafe, named "The Rim," squats humbly at the side of the road in Heber. If you're in the neighborhood of a morning, try breakfast. Inside, the place is clean and the chow, delicious. That is, if you cotton to biscuits 'n' gravy, chicken-fried steak,

and Denver omelets. Check out the bottle, tool, barbed wire, and pioneer portrait collections. Heber and satellite Overgaard have become service centers for hundreds of summer and retirement homes gracing the ridges and lining the shallow draws. While a thousand feet lower than the edge of the Rim, Heber still averages somewhat cooler temperatures than Payson.

Founded as a Mormon colony in 1876-77, Heber

Once a deep, rugged, remote chasm carved into the Colorado Plateau, Woods Canyon now contains an artificial lake that has offered fishing and boating for a generation of recreationists. The Woods Canyon Lake Recreation Area offers camping, RV services, boat rentals, groceries, beverages, and almost anything else the camper needs.
NICK BEREZENKO

maintains its village facade of industrious clutter and goes about its ranching, distribution, and retail businesses with the confident attitude of people living within their means.

Some years Heber also throws one of Arizona's best summertime, small-town rodeos. Elsewhere, big-time cowboy tournaments are diluted by circus acts and glittering balladeers. When Heber competes, and at other towns on and under the Rim, rodeo casually survives in its original forms — riding, roping, and wrestling.

East of Overgaard about a mile, begins a trip back to the violent history of the Old West. Just after crossing Pierce Wash, turn south off State Route 260 on Forest Service Road 144 for 2.8 miles. This is a good-weather road. At FR 124, turn west and go a half mile. Turn south on FR 125 and go 2.6 miles to a large meadow which opens on your left — Phoenix Park.

It was named by James Stinson who owned the land and ran cattle on it in 1882. He had a home in Phoenix and applied that name here. Stinson ran cattle in the Rim country as early as 1873 and owned a ranch to the north on Silver Creek, which he sold to Mormon colonists who there founded the town of Snowflake.

Rustlers fighting over absentee-owner Stinson's herds led to one of the West's bloodiest range feuds, known as the Pleasant Valley War.

Before and after Stinson, Phoenix Park acquired a colorful history. General George Crook bivouacked his troops in this meadow during his Indian campaign. After Stinson, Daniel Boone Holcomb and his wife acquired the ranch at Phoenix Park (some maps still call the place Holcomb). The Holcombs died, leaving their 14-year-old daughter. Sarah stayed on, ranching her entire life.

Today, elk bed down in the grassy meadow, a small spring seeps beneath giant cottonwoods on the west side, and the fireplace and foundation of Sarah's ranch house still stands. The ruins highlight a stroll around the large clearing.

Continue south two miles to FR 300, drive west 12 miles to Gentry Lookout, then a little less than two miles to the trailhead to where frontier justice failed (starts on the east side of Black Canyon Rim Campground).

Sometimes out West, they hanged the wrong men.

That happened atop the Rim more than a century ago. Three suspected horse thieves swung from the same tree . . . from the same limb.

The incident grew out of the Pleasant Valley War, which Zane Grey borrowed from for his novel *To the Last Man*. But no writer of fiction could rival the raw violence of this range war, also known as the Graham-Tewksbury Feud.

For 15 years, from the early 1880s to the late 1890s, the war crackled around the Rim country like Mogollon sheet lightning. And before it wound down, certainly 30 men were dead. Possibly as many as 50. Thumbnails of the more sensational episodes:

Men were wounded as early as 1883, but the first to die was a shepherd in January, 1887, apparently assassinated while camped north of Pleasant Valley. The Navajo herder was beheaded — perhaps as a warning to all sheepmen.

On a Sunday afternoon, September 4, 1887, in a one-street railroad stop named Holbrook north of the Rim, Sheriff Commodore Perry Owens (Commodore was his first name) stomped up onto the porch of a tiny frame house and demanded the surrender of one alleged rustler, Andy Cooper. By the time the gunfire ceased 30 seconds later, Cooper and two other men were fatally shot and a fourth was crippled for life.

In the summer of 1888, the bushwhacking of Pleasant Valley settlers so intensified that the residents huddled together in a meadow commune, while two battle-ready companies of U.S. troops took up protective positions.

The last Graham to die was Tom. He was shot in the back (August 2, 1892) while driving a wagon load of grain to Tempe. His young widow concealed his sixshooter in her handbag, and when the courtroom was concentrating on testimony at a hearing for the alleged killer, she shoved the pistol into the side of the suspect and pulled the trigger. Misfire. The hammer caught on a fold of cloth.

The triple hanging atop the Rim was of still another kind of tragedy. James Stott, free-spirited, 25-year-old son of a prominent Massachusetts family, had established a horse ranch north of the Rim near Bear Springs. Generous financial support flowed from his parents. He had no need of other money. Had no cause to steal. Probably, he crossed harm's way when northern Arizona sheepmen began to covet his water and range.

Sheepman and Deputy J.D. Houck and a small

Stott, Scott, and Wilson Gravesite Trail Information

DIFFICULTY: Easy to moderate, rocky in places.
TRAIL ACCESS: On State Route 260, go 0.2 mile east of Milepost 291, turn south on FR 300, and go 2.8 miles to the trailhead sign on the north side of the road just past Black Canyon Rim Campground.

ELEVATION: 7,600 feet.
DISTANCE: 0.7 mile one way.
HIKING TIME: 45 minutes round trip.
SEASON: April-November.
MARKED: Oak trail signs and blue diamond markers.
WATER: None.
PARKING: Roadside at trailhead.
CONTACT: Black Mesa Ranger District, (520) 535-4481.

For a more detailed account of this hanging and the Pleasant Valley War, read *A Little War of Our Own*, by Don Dedera. The out-of-print book can be found through used-book dealers.

posse surprised and arrested Jamie Stott and two cabin guests, Jim Scott and Billy Wilson, at Stott's Circle Dot Ranch headquarters at dawn on August 11, 1888 (not August 4, as on the modern headstones). The posse charged the three with horse theft. The doomed men were put on horses and carried westward several miles when a large band of vigilantes called the "Committee of 50" intercepted the posse. The Committee took charge of the handcuffed and chained men, ran off the small posse, and continued westward on the Old Verde Road. (Old Verde Road, FR 166, is suitable for four-wheel-drive only. See map, pages 32-33.) They lynched the young men near present-day Black Canyon Rim Campground. All three bodies were found days later, hanging from one stout bough of a ponderosa pine, and were buried there in the forest.

Every effort by Stott's parents to bring the vigilantes to justice was foiled by friends of the vigilantes. The perpetrators were never punished, except, perhaps, in their nightmares.

A short hike on a well-marked trail leads to the lovely glade where these men found their final rest.

From the gravesite trailhead, continue northwest on FR 300 to State Route 260. Turn left, west, go two miles to Forest Lakes, and turn north on FR 99.

Down and up, up and down. Think of two dozen baguettes of French bread, lying side by side . . . and together tilted slightly upward at one end. The long loaves make rounded ridges north and south, divided by ravines, the higher ends joined at the Rim. Now multiply your imagery by thousands. The mass of baguettes is the plateau, gently dropping down to the sagebrush flats of Coconino and Apache counties.

We begin our next driving adventure at Forest Lakes Estates. FR 99 heads north just a quarter-mile west of the gas station. Almost immediately, half-hidden cabins give way to open greens mingling with clusters of conifers. Squirrels undulate out front,

(OPPOSITE PAGE) Most prominent remnant of Sarah Holcomb's homestead at Phoenix Park is her chimney. WILLIAM E. BARCUS
(UPPER LEFT) The shaded graves of Stott, Scott, and Wilson. WESLEY HOLDEN
(ABOVE LEFT) A black bear (cinnamon type) lumbers through ponderosa pine woodlands near West Clear Creek. WILLIAM E. BARCUS
(ABOVE RIGHT) A fat mule deer doe. WILLIAM E. BARCUS

and a gilded flicker flashes over our hood. At 3.7 miles from the State 260 turnoff, take a sharp left turn onto FR 170 and into specimen pines preserved as seedstock following recent logging. Arizona forests have never been clear-cut, and in this timber sale, the trimmings (slash) are stacked for burning in a safer season. Soon a fresh generation of seedlings will replace the harvest. Never, ever, has the Forest Service planted so many trees as in recent years.

Then, there! To the left! Twelve elk cows with their maturing young lope like a freight train through the glen. My companion, an Eastern-raised woman, may have a heart attack.

"These are part of a 10,000 herd," I say, as the elk keep pace with our Blazer. "They're on the increase. It's one of America's ecological tragedy/victory stories. During frontier times, the original Merriam elk gave way to human occupation of the Rim country. They disappeared. Hunting? Loss of range to cow grazing? Introduced disease? Those elk over there are the descendants of several transplants of Rocky Mountain elk from Yellowstone between 1913 and 1928."

There is not much difference in appearance between the two elk types. We groan when our road bends away from the cruising herd. They, in their flanking maneuver, had given not one inch of ground.

It is a little more than nine miles from the highway to FR 90. We decide to take a side trip. From here on it's a four-wheel-drive and high-center road.

Since we have the appropriate vehicle, we follow George Pemberton's advice and slowly grind four miles northwest to Weimer Point (at 0.5 mile take the right fork, at 2.5 miles, the left).

We pass through the eastern portion of the 4,000-acre Slim Fire. It is interesting to see how quickly the forest is recovering since the campfire-caused blaze swept through the area July 4, 1987. We park in a convenient turnaround area and walk the last 0.3 mile, as the rough road becomes more like a trail.

Abruptly, Chevelon Canyon Lake appears: a glistening blue surprise, where eagles soar on thermal currents, and with binoculars you can look for big fish lolling in the shallows. If your car can't take a rough road, consider parking it and then walk in and out. It takes a good half day (take water) and makes a great picnic hike.

Proceeding north on FR 170 toward Chevelon Crossing, we drive slowly, watching for deer, turkey, or javelina to cross the gravel road. The land continues to lose elevation and pines give way to cedar breaks. Just before linking up with FR 504 and turning west, an extensive example of juniper eradication

(ABOVE) This spectacular overlook awaits adventurers who hike or four-wheel drive to Weimer Point above Chevelon Canyon Lake. The lake, however, is inaccessible from this point.
(OPPOSITE PAGE) Waders and anglers test the placid Chevelon Creek at historic Chevelon Crossing.
PHOTOS BY NICK BEREZENKO

As we wind our way up the west side of the canyon, we pass a small campground with ramadas and table-bench units. Perfect for the camper/fisherman. Just past the crest of the hill, on the left, a track leads off to the remains of the CCC camp that once housed the young men who built this road, bridge, and campground.

At 26 miles is FR 169, and we turn sharply left. Now heading southwest, the road begins to climb and the scenery is reversed, from scrubby cedars and piñons we nuzzle back into the big pines. Piñon jays. Indian paintbrush. More deer. And then we link up with FR 300, the General Crook Trail, at aptly named Alder Lake for a total of 47 miles. What a day.

But in the opinion of others, there are even better days, days of autumn color. One morning all is green; next day, among the evergreens, a riot of leathery browns, ruby, saffron, crimson, burgundy. Scrub oaks tint entire slopes. Aspens splurge their gold dollars. Sumacs blaze. Elders wax flaxen. It was Albert Camus who said: "Autumn is a second spring when every leaf is a flower."

There exists a human scale and perspective in autumn that is somehow diminished in the gaudy promise of spring and the gross plenitude of summer. Here, between first frost and first snowfall, likely live the greatest percentage of people who don't give a hoot if the dollar buys fewer yen, if neckties narrow or widen, or if civilization elsewhere declines. It is time to core an apple and think a worthwhile thought. ◙

dominates the landscape. It is done to give range grass a better chance.

Because of steep hairpin turns, this road is limited to vehicles no more than 35 feet long. The narrow road's washboard surface dictates slow speed down to the one-lane bridge over the placid stream, where three trucks are parked. They are the only vehicles we have seen all morning. From the highway at Forest Lakes, it is 24 miles to the wrinkled canyon walls at Chevelon Crossing (not including the side trip to Weimer Point).

RIM LAKES

When Europeans first arrived, Arizona had but one permanent lake — a basin of snowmelt inside a collapsed volcano near Flagstaff. Today, there are some 200 sizeable artificial reservoirs within the state. They range from vast inland seas, like Lake Powell, to municipal water impoundments, but none is more handsome than the Rim's string of small recreational lakes.

Bear Canyon Lake — Not much used, Bear Canyon is many an avid angler's favorite. The well-built but steep trail discourages the faint of heart and weak of leg. Fishing is limited to flies and artificial lures. Sixty acres of turquoise water hold rainbow and brook trout, some cutthroat and arctic grayling. Strict fishing regulations apply. The pretty, dispersed camping area is ringed by aspens. Access: Take State Route 260 to the Woods Canyon Lake turnoff, then west on Forest Service Road 300 for 15 miles to FR 89. Go north three miles to the lake site entrance, then switchback a mile to the head of the lake.

Black Canyon Lake — A continuation of unpaved FR 300 leaves State Route 260 at 0.2 mile east of Milepost 291, which is about two miles east of Forest Lakes Estates. The road can be slick and muddy after rains. Bank-casting after rainbow and brown trout is customary. There's a paved ramp and the Black Canyon Rim Campground, 21 units, is about two miles from the lake.

Blue Ridge Reservoir — A commercial purpose justified a dam at the confluence of East Clear Creek and General Springs Canyon. A 160-foot-high concrete barrel-arch structure, the first of its kind in the United States, forms a narrow lake. When full, Blue Ridge Reservoir covers more than 200 acres. The deal between Phelps Dodge and the Salt River Project allowed the mining firm to take project water in eastern Arizona and pay it back with water from north of the Rim. Two bonuses: The pay-back water runs down the East Verde, ensuring a strong, steady flow; and the reservoir affords splendid recreation, including fishing for rainbows and a few big brownies. Nearby campgrounds include 10-unit Blue Ridge, 7-unit Clints Well, and 35-unit Rock Crossing. (See map, pages 32-33) Access: State Route 87, 4.5 miles north of Clint's Well; the good but unpaved FR 751 goes about six miles east to the reservoir.

Chevelon Lake — This is one of the largest and most difficult to get to of all the Rim lakes. Its nearly

200 acres wind through incredibly beautiful steep canyon walls for nearly three miles. When dam construction was started in the early 1960s, the first order of business was building a road to the site. Since the dam was completed, the road has slowly deteriorated until now it is only a trail. Even FR 169B, which takes visitors and fisherman past Chevelon Lake Campground on the top of the canyon, is difficult, almost impossible in stormy conditions. Access: From State Route 260, take Woods Canyon Lake turnoff and go eight miles westerly on FR 300 to FR 169. Turn right, northeasterly, driving 11.5 miles to FR 169B, the Chevelon Lake turnoff, then 1.5 miles to the parking area. From there, it's a steep one-mile walk on a well-marked trail to the lake.

Knoll Lake — A high lake at 7,900 feet, Knoll extends two arms to cover 75 acres of East Leonard Canyon. Its name comes from a little, knoll-like island, ideal for picnicking. As in most Rim country lakes, stocked rainbow trout far outnumber big browns. Only electric trolling motors are allowed. Knoll Lake Campground, 33 units, usually is uncrowded Monday through Thursday, but jampacked on summer weekends. Access: FR 295E branches off from FR 300 about 24 miles west of State Route 260. The road to the lake is 4.5 miles long and rough.

Willow Springs Lake — The epitome of easy access, a paved road at Milepost 283 on State Route 260 leads 1.4 miles to the 80-acre lake. A paved ramp facilitates launching boats with motors of not more than eight horsepower. The quarry: rainbow and brown trout (some big ones). Sink Hole Campground, 26 units, is less than a mile away.

Woods Canyon Lake — The beginning of the Rim's bounteous artificial recreation lakes, 52-acre Woods Canyon was dammed in 1956 and filled that winter. It has become one of Arizona's most popular and best developed water recreation areas: with a store, boat rental, picnic area, five large-to-medium campgrounds, an encircling hike and a nature trail. Catchable trout are stocked directly from the hatchery. Access: State Route 260 east of Payson to the Woods Canyon Lake turnoff at the top of the Rim. From there, it's five paved miles to the lake.

A raft drifts across Willow Springs Lake while folks on the shore enjoy fishing and picnicking.
BOB CLEMENZ

Chapter Six

One of the very first travelers across the Rim was a remarkable woman. In the late summer of 1872, Martha Summerhayes joined her soldier husband and rode in a military wagon (called an ambulance) from Fort Mohave on the Colorado River to the territorial capital of Prescott, then continued 150 miles farther eastward across the Rim country to Fort Apache. At the time, she was six months pregnant.

Many years later, safe in her New England home, she gathered up her notes and recollections and wrote her classic memoir, *Vanished Arizona*.

The initial 40-mile pull from Prescott to Fort Verde, on the Verde River, was a walk in the park, but from there the "road" was all but impassable. It heaved and curved to Thirteen Mile Rock where a ramp only slightly wider than the wagon track literally had been carved into the face of that solid monolith. The grade was so steep that soldiers had to throw their shoulders into the wheels to assist the mules that already were double- and triple-teamed.

Martha Summerhayes wrote in 1908: "The traveling was very difficult and rough, and both men and animals were

West Atop The Rim

WHERE THE FIRST WHEELS TURNED

worn out by night. But we were now in the mountains, the air was cool and pleasant, and the nights so cold that we were glad to have a small stove in our tents to dress by in the mornings. The scenery was wild and grand; in fact, beyond all that I had ever dreamed of; more than that, it seemed so untrod, so fresh, somehow, and I do not suppose that even now, in the day of railroads and tourists, many people have had the view of the Tonto Basin which we had one day from

(OPPOSITE PAGE) Quaking aspens don their autumn dress. Beavers used to dam the waters of Bear Canyon atop the Rim. Today, a bigger dam, built by humans, transforms the canyon into a fly fisherman's paradise.
(RIGHT) Mountain bicycling offers a different way to negotiate the Woods Canyon Lake Trail.
PHOTOS BY NICK BEREZENKO

the top of the Mogollon range." The cavalcade fed itself from the land: antelope, turkey, deer. Martha Summerhayes and her trooper Jack reached Fort Apache after two months of continuous travel.

Today, this journey over General Crook's road conceivably could be accomplished in a few hours by passenger car — more remarkable in that contemporary highways and byways closely follow the original. You may also find remarkable that the appearance of the land and its life are so similar to those of 120 years ago. Thanks for this belongs in large measure to the setting aside as undeveloped public lands the Coconino National Forest, encompassing the Mogollon Plateau on the west, and Apache and Sitgreaves national forests on the east.

In the Rim country, Forest Service Road 300, improved in 1928, frequently intersects Crook's old military road. In

common with the old, the newer, better graded but still unpaved route dips and weaves across the densely wooded Mogollon, here leaving the Rim to visit fir-and-aspen glades, there skirting the very edge of the plateau. Out there was where Capt. George M. Wheeler marveled:

"Mountain, forest, valley, and streams are blended in one harmonious whole . . . few worldwide travelers in a lifetime could be treated to a more perfect landscape, a true virgin solitude, undefiled by the presence of man."

The military road was the strategic penetration of the most remote realm of the fierce Apaches, who in their zenith terrorized a region larger than Germany and France combined. Over this crucial supply line Gen. George C. Crook not only supported distant outposts, but dropped off fighting units to raid Apache camps throughout Tonto Basin. It required a decade of intense campaigning, but in the end, no Apache haven was secure from the troops and Indian scouts faithfully serving General Crook. Out of respect, the Apaches gave Crook the name Gray Wolf.

The green, young enlisted men who scratched the road across the Rim measured miles by counting

the revolutions of a wagon wheel. Every time a white-painted spoke came around, a soldier dropped a pebble into a bucket. At each mile, they chiseled the number into a boulder or carved it into a tree. The vast wildness of the Mogollon Rim and the threat of Indian attack worried these young men who were mostly from the East or had recently immigrated from Europe. To ensure they didn't lose their way, these raw recruits blazed a remarkable number of trees along the trail at intervals so close a blaze was never out of sight. The dot-dash, like an inverted exclamation point on the fronts and backs of trees on both sides of the road, showed the way.

Numerous blazed trees, ancient even then, still line the road, which in sections faintly shows as ruts

(LEFT) On his favorite mule, Maude, Gen. George C. Crook campaigned with his Apache Indian scouts. COURTESY ARIZONA HISTORICAL SOCIETY
(ABOVE) Split rail fence, Kehl Springs Campground. NICK BEREZENKO
(OPPOSITE PAGE) The word "vertical" assumes full meaning on the edge of the Rim at Hi View Point. NICK BEREZENKO
(FOLLOWING PANEL) South from the Rim, seven distinct ridgelines can be counted. DICK DIETRICH

across slickrock and shallow cuts along slopes. In 1975, the Boy Scouts of Northern Arizona adopted the Crook Trail as their Bicentennial project. Where many markings were missing, scout troops erected posts bearing chevrons. They also placed chevrons on surviving blazed trees, so that every one of the 135 miles of public land that Crook's road traverses is marked for you.

FR 300 is the east-west connector from which scores of other forest roads and foot trails head north or south. Generally north-running routes head gently downhill through a swatch of forest 20 to 30 miles wide. Southerly foot trails drop steeply off the Rim. FR 300 wants to be driven leisurely, going easy on the springs, tires, and passengers. Some of the roads that branch northward are better negotiated in four-wheel-drive or high-clearance truck. And where the runoff gathers and cuts deep canyons in its rush to the Colorado River, some ways are simply not passable. It pays to inquire locally, particularly in wet seasons.

With that caveat, here are some things to do and places to visit on the western portion of the Mogollon Rim.

Blue Ridge Reservoir, Knoll Lake, and Bear Canyon Lake — (For complete information, see "Rim Lakes Guide," pages 52-53.)

Barbershop Canyon — As one admirer has written, "This canyon contains more wildlife than many zoos." Several roads and hiking trails descend the ledges of this scenic canyon, and other paths lead to Dick Hart and Dane ridges. Because of the elemental land forms and changeable road conditions, it's best to inquire at the Happy Jack Information Center located at Milepost 290 on State Route 87, south of the intersection with Forest Highway 3; (520) 477-2172. The rewards are worth the effort, but clambering about this bit of backwoods requires smart planning and reasonably good health.

Baker Butte Fire Tower — Exactly 10.4 miles north of Strawberry, State Route 87 crosses the General Crook Trail (FR 300). Then 1.4 miles east, FR 300 leads to a right turnoff through a gate. Climb rocky switchbacks to the top of the butte. At 8,034 feet, this is the highest point on the Rim. In low gear, you will urge your vehicle along forest floors lush with fern, wild strawberry, columbine, and cliff rose. Oaks and conifers crowd the narrow canyons

and march along the ridges to the clearing around the tower. There's been a lookout on Baker Butte since the teen years of the 20th century, when men with binoculars perched on the limb of a pine and shouted alarms over a rudimentary telephone. If the guard is not busy, you may go up. To the southwest, the Mazatzal Mountains block the view of Camelback Mountain in Phoenix, but southeasterly, on crystal clear days, you can see the top of the Santa Catalina Mountains at Tucson. Look north and see the Hopi mesas. In all, the view totals 250 miles! Tiny but beautiful 8-unit Kehl Springs Campground is nearby.

The Cabin Loop Trails — Connecting three early-day Forest Service cabins with pathways and telephone lines, the loop once fed fire alerts and other information to the Long Valley Ranger Station. The loop and surviving structures today lie within

for General Crook. *Arizona Highways* writer James E. Cook, who in the 1940s lived in this cabin for five summers while his dad worked for the Forest Service, cherishes warm memories: "That log house was about 25 years old when we lived there. It was a cozy home, especially in the evening when we read or played cards by the light of a Coleman lantern or listened to Fibber McGee on the battery-powered radio. The outhouse was over the hill. We carried water in galvanized pails from the spring, 50 yards from the cabin." In 1989, the Forest Service restored the structure. Access: From State Route 87, go east 12 miles on FR 300. The cabin is only a half mile north of FR 300.

Buck Springs Fire Guard Station — Two cabins, one dating to 1923, are still used during high-risk months by firefighters. Only the site remains of the very first Buck Springs cabin built in the early

the Blue Ridge Ranger District. At elevations around 7,500 feet, the Cabin Loop Trails circulate through some of the plateau's most spectacular scenery: ever-flowing springs, diverse geological features, and rich foliage. The trails cross miles of forest terrain and are not for the inexperienced hiker. For more information on these trails, contact the Happy Jack Information Center or buy "The Mogollon Rim Hiking Map" from *Arizona Highways*, 2039 West Lewis Avenue, Phoenix, AZ 85009, (800) 543-5432.

If hiking is not an option for you, you can drive to each of the cabins.

General Springs Cabin — The place was named

1900s. Access: From FR 300, go is 4.2 miles via FR 137, turn right, and go 0.7 mile on FR 137D.

Pinchot Cabin — Gifford Pinchot (1865-1946) was a trailblazing forester and conservationist who led the U.S. Forest Service from 1898 to 1910, inspiring many of its early conservation policies. After he visited the site and remarked upon its beauty, foresters named the place after him. Several now-vanished cabins preceded this one, built in the 1930s by a fire guard. Access: Take State 87 to Blue Ridge Ranger Station, go 11 miles south on FR 95, then left on FR 139A for 0.2 mile. Pinchot Cabin will be on your left.

(OPPOSITE PAGE, LEFT) Along the Cabin Loop Trail, hikers encounter this old line shack of a ranching operation. WILLIAM E. BARCUS
(OPPOSITE PAGE, RIGHT) Long and very deep, Blue Ridge Reservoir was created to effect a water trade from one Rim country drainage to another. WILLARD CLAY
(ABOVE) Massive rock formations await hikers to West Clear Creek Wilderness. NICK BEREZENKO

West Clear Creek Wilderness — Road access to this wilderness area is difficult, and the steep hiking trail even more so. With preparation and care, experienced outdoorspeople will find West Clear Creek amply rewarding, with fern-covered grottoes, deep crystalline pools, and springs protected from the rest of the world by 700-foot-high canyon walls. Go fully prepared, and be sure someone on the outside knows where you're going. An accident here would leave you *very* alone. Access to the Maxwell Trailhead: Take State 87 to Clints Well, then go north on Forest Highway 3 about seven miles to the West Clear Creek sign. Go west on FR 81

another seven miles (go straight ahead on FR 81E when the road splits) until the pavement stops. Turn left to the end of the road (this section may need four-wheel drive). The trailhead is marked with a sign and rock cairn. It is recommended you contact Happy Jack Information Center before entering the wilderness area.

Battle of Big Dry Wash — It was the last pitched battle between substantial numbers of Apaches and U.S. troops.

In late spring, 1882, firebrand Nan-tia-tish and his band bolted from the San Carlos Apache reservation and raided below the Rim in Pleasant Valley. They stole horses, killed prospectors, wounded ranchers, and burned buildings. A few days later, with as many as 250 warriors, Nan-tia-tish beset the Meadows Ranch on the East Verde. They killed the father and wounded two sons, one fatally.

But the warriors' days were numbered. U.S. military forces converged from several directions. Feeling invincible, however, the renegades dawdled northward. By July 16, soldiers from five Arizona army posts pressed the renegades up onto the Tonto Rim. Suspecting a trap near General Springs, the soldiers set one of their own. With Maj. Adna R. Chaffee as battle commander, the soldiers and their Indian scouts on July 17 baited the Apaches with a column of cavalry on white horses. Then while the Indians were distracted, other units outflanked them down Battleground Ridge.

In the ensuing close-quarter combat, Apache fatalities numbered about 22. On the army side, one Apache scout was killed and several soldiers wounded. Had not a severe, high-country thunder and hail storm obscured the battlefield for 20 minutes, Indian losses surely would have been greater.

The battle area is honored by a roadside monument, but historians now are convinced the actual battle occurred on the ridge across the canyon from the marker. For many years, the ground all about was littered by spent ammunition, broken equipment, and the ration containers that gave the area its name of Crackerbox Canyon. ◪

Battle of Big Dry Wash Trail Information

DIFFICULTY: Easy.

TRAIL ACCESS: Take FR 300 about 11.8 miles east from State Route 87, then follow the signs north on FR 123 about seven miles, taking the left fork where indicated. The monument is 0.25 mile beyond the road's end. The actual battle area is another 0.5 mile beyond.

ELEVATION: 7,000 - 6,600 feet.

DISTANCE: 0.75 mile one way.

HIKING TIME: 45 minutes round trip.

SEASON: May-October.

SIGNAGE: Lack of a sign makes the trailhead a little difficult to find, but the trail is easy to follow. There are two bronze plaques at the monument.

WATER: None.

PARKING: Roadside at end of road.

CONTACT: Happy Jack Information Center, (520) 477-2172.

W H E N   Y O U   G O . . .

Between Strawberry and Coconino National Forest's northern boundary, roadside services are few along State 87's scenic solitude. About midway, the little community of Clints Well offers food and fuel. From its nearby junction with State 87, Forest Highway 3 presents a handsome high-country drive northwestward past several big lakes to Flagstaff.

Happy Jack Information Center
(Coconino National Forest) At Clints Well, Milepost 290 on State Route 87. (520) 477-2172.

Coconino National Forest
2323 East Greenlaw Lane, Flagstaff.
(520) 556-7400
Web site: www.fs.fed.us/r3/coconino/

Arizona Game & Fish Department
2222 West Greenway Road, Phoenix. For fishing reports and licenses, wildlife recovery programs, boating registration, etc. (602) 942-3000   Web site: www.gf.state.az.us/

(LEFT) Clints Well, where Forest Highway 3 joins State Route 87, offers Rim country adventurers an outpost in the vast expanses of Coconino National Forest.
(OPPOSITE PAGE) Mouth of the Mineral Belt Railroad Tunnel.
PHOTOS BY NICK BEREZENKO

One of Arizona's oddest early-day episodes involved big dreams, daring gambles, high hopes, numbing toil, and ultimate defeat.

The scheme to pierce the Mogollon Rim with a railroad tunnel was the brainchild of Chicago attorney and entrepreneur James W. Eddy. In its most grandiose extension, the Arizona Mineral Belt Railroad would traverse the entirety of the territory, south to north, from the Mexican border near Nogales to the Utah border near Lees Ferry. By intersecting with the Southern Pacific Railroad in the south and the Atlantic & Pacific in the north, the Mineral Belt would transform Tucson and Flagstaff into major railroad hubs.

Those were the easy parts.

The tough nut to crack: the Mogollon Rim.

But capital was raised, and engineers advanced a plan. A bore of 3,100 feet, 16 feet wide at the bottom and 20 feet high, would take advantage of a natural notch in the Rim north of Payson. The anticipated destination through the sandstone was General Springs Canyon atop the Rim.

A crew of 40 began work in August, 1883. In little more than a month, the drillers made 70 feet of tunnel. Then, Eddy ran out of money, and work stopped.

Over the next decade, an agony of refinancing, tracklaying, backstabbing, and suing plagued the Mineral Belt Railroad project. The grand concept finally was abandoned, leaving a few miles of roadbed on fairly level ground near Flagstaff and this tunnel going nowhere on the Rim. ⚑

Railroad Tunnel Trail Information

DIFFICULTY: Difficult, steep with loose footing in places.

TRAIL ACCESS: Take FR 300 east, 12 miles from its junction with State Route 87 to the Battle of Big Dry Wash monument. Start at the small trailhead sign on the south side of FR 300. Following power lines, descend 100 feet, then turn left at the second power pole to join the trail down the east side of the canyon. Continue approximately 0.5 mile to the next small sign where the trail fishhooks to the left and starts back up the Rim to the tunnel. This last 0.25 mile of trail is steep, very rocky, and somewhat difficult to follow.

ELEVATION: 7,200 feet.

DISTANCE: 1.5 miles round trip.

HIKING TIME: Two to three hours.

SIGNAGE: Small trail signs.

WATER: None.

PARKING: Roadside at Battle of Big Dry Wash monument.

SEASONS: April-November.

CONTACT: Payson Ranger District, (520) 474-7900; Happy Jack Information Center, (520) 477-2172.

For a more complete story, see "A Vision of Grandeur: The Arizona Mineral Belt Railroad," by Robert A. Trennert, in *Arizona and the West* (Winter, 1970), a scholarly quarterly published by the University of Arizona Press.

ABOUT MOUNTAIN DRIVING

FRANK ZULLO

Arizona's uplands are crisscrossed by modern motoring routes, from four-lane highways to four-wheel-drive trails. Here are some tips:

Stay tuned to weather news — At higher elevations, Arizona's climate is wetter, cooler, and stormier than the low deserts. Wind gusts can give high-profile vehicles trouble. Unpaved roads can become slick and gummy after rain showers and snow thaws.

Slow down — Inquire locally about road conditions.

Take chains or snow tires — The state highway patrol often requires drivers to use them from October through April when slush or ice slicken blacktop. Back roads can become partly frozen quagmires.

Check automobile fluids — Daytime temperatures may drop as much as 40 degrees after sunset. Liquid-cooled engines need antifreeze protection during colder seasons. So does your windshield washing water.

Top off your gas tank — Uphill driving can double fuel consumption. In places, it's a far piece between service stations.

Learn the log truck duck — It's a handy maneuver for defensive driving on unpaved roads. On sighting an approaching rig, slow down, skirt to the right side, and pray that a flying stone will not ding your windshield.

Beware of creek crossings — This means even dry ones. Flash flooding can result from faraway storms that you may not see.

Be alert — Wildlife and range cattle frequent roadways, often at night.

Share your plans — Tell a responsible party about your itinerary, especially when hiking. If you don't show up, they'll know where to search.